Historical Heroines

100 Women You Should Know About

Michelle Rosenberg and Sonia D. Picker

PEN & SWORD
HISTORY

First published in Great Britain in 2018 by
PEN AND SWORD HISTORY
an imprint of
Pen and Sword Books Ltd
47 Church Street
Barnsley
South Yorkshire S70 2AS

ISBN 978 1 52671 533 3

Printed and bound by CPI Group (UK) Ltd, Croydon, CR0 4YY

Typeset in Times New Roman by
Aura Technology and Software Services, India

Pen & Sword Books Ltd incorporates the imprints of Pen & Sword
Archaeology, Atlas, Aviation, Battleground, Discovery,
Family History, History, Maritime, Military, Naval, Politics, Railways,
Select, Social History, Transport, True Crime, Claymore Press,
Frontline Books, Leo Cooper, Praetorian Press, Remember When,
Seaforth Publishing and Wharncliffe.

For a complete list of Pen and Sword titles please contact
Pen and Sword Books Limited
47 Church Street, Barnsley, South Yorkshire, S70 2AS, England
E-mail: enquiries@pen-and-sword.co.uk
Website: www.pen-and-sword.co.uk

Contents

Preface

I am so glad that there is finally a book specifically addressing the issue of women who have been sidelined from history via slandering, being demeaned or simply ignored.

I am a direct descendant of both Dame Emma Hamilton (yes, her correct title is Dame and equal to Nelson's) and Nelson's sister, Kitty Matcham, through the cousins' marriage of their grandchildren William George Ward and Catherine Blanckley.

The extent to which Emma herself has been slandered, demeaned and ignored is staggering. She was the first English woman to be awarded the Maltese Cross for bravery. She played a huge role in supporting Britain in its war efforts against France and invented an entirely new art form, and yet she has largely been remembered as 'that harlot who seduced Nelson'.

Many people can't even let mention of her name pass without berating the injustice served to Nelson's wife, Fanny, by their affair – although these same people never bring the issue of Fanny up when Nelson is mentioned.

I founded the Emma Hamilton Society to champion her cause. However, even Kitty Matcham, my lesser known fourth great-grandmother, has lately been subjected to slander albeit along with her husband, George. Bountiful evidence shows the couple to have been unwaveringly loyal to Emma throughout her long and fatal decline, supporting her financially and even fostering her teenaged daughter after Emma's death in 1815. However, the Matchams have recently been portrayed as penniless scroungers who unscrupulously preyed on Emma's gullibility. I feel a protective sense of duty towards the Matchams and all those people, many of whom are women, unjustly sidelined from history.

I welcome this book as a long awaited voice for them.

Lily Style
April 2018

Introduction – Sonia D. Picker

Writing and cooking at the same time.

My mum cooked from memory, gorgeous meals that were an absolute treat. And then she got ill and then she died. Her recipes are lost forever as I never wrote them down and was too interested in hanging out with my friends when I had the chance to learn from her. They are gone and a part of her is gone. Sad is too inadequate a word.

And this is how we and all future generations should feel about all our ancestors and the oceans of information lost to time: medicines, art, fiction, inventions, tales of heroism, inspiration. All gone because half the human race decided the other half were inconsequential and none of this was ever written down – again sad is inadequate.

And look at what little we do have recorded . . .

Nowadays we talk about spectrums. We used to talk about shades of grey before its associations made us giggle about red rooms and spanking. The point is we know, and always have, that the human character is complex. Very few, if any, people are completely evil or 100 per cent good. So why, for the love of god, have women been written about in history like a bad bi-polar cliché – the virgin Madonna vs the sexually deviant demon. It's just so boring

Anyone who has studied history and been lectured about the importance of primary sources ad nauseum can only wonder at the liberties our ye olde historians took. Writing years after the lives of their subjects (victims), much of the documented detail seemed to owe more to their sordid imaginations than to old fashioned evidence.

Few women in history have been credited with actually being a real human with all the complexities and shades that brings. In every era of history, they have been polarised: the benevolent, self-sacrificing angel mother or sexually perverse, power grabbing, demon baby eater. Their lives reduced to the type of black and white thinking that belongs to tantruming toddlers.

The purpose of this book is not just to celebrate the female heroines missing, misunderstood or hidden in the footnotes of history books. We want to bask in all the layers a woman has, from the remarkable to the despicable.

HISTORICAL HEROINES

This is a lighthearted glimpse at some of these women, many of whom will be familiar in their native countries and celebrated in folklore legend but who deserve a wider audience.

It may seem an arbitrary mix that we have chosen but we delved into the growing pile of women's history and selected those gals we felt were missing from most lists or had been miscast and misunderstood. Above all, we hope our brief dalliances with their lives are interesting, compelling and fun. I suspect we will suffer the same fate as every other top 100 list you see in the media from films to sex toys – these lists are ubiquitous and of course, totally, subjective. We know there are thousands more that could have been included but it's a short book and we could only pick 100. What unites our cast of characters is that they have all suffered being miscast, typecast or simply cast aside.

Introduction – Michelle Rosenberg

The premise of this book is simple. We wanted to serve up 100 women that you absolutely need to know about.

Sure, there's bound to be the few women you always learn about at school. But there's a hell of a lot more out there that deserve their place in the spotlight.

We've got quite a global cast for you; there are those whose lives are missing from traditional history books (that would be around 95 per cent then). Those whose lives and legacies have been misunderstood. Overlooked. Defined purely by the men in their lives. Taken a back seat to their husbands' achievements. Unjustly maligned. And had their lives unfairly edited by ancient (and not-so ancient) historians (probably men).

You can understand that keeping this book to just 100 profiles was a struggle. But we figured that any more miscast, missing and misunderstood women in one sitting might push you over the edge in your righteous, indignant fury. So actually, we're thinking of you. (You're welcome.)

It may seem we've chosen an arbitrary mix but we just delved into our growing pile of women's history and selected those gals we felt were interesting, compelling or just fun. These lists are ubiquitous and, of course, totally subjective. We know there are thousands more that could have been included. What unites our cast of characters is that they have all suffered being miscast, typecast or simply cast aside.

So, sit back. Read. Enjoy. And kick some butt in solidarity.

Ada Blackjack
(1898–29 May 1983)

Ada Blackjack was labelled the female Robinson Crusoe but whilst he was a work of fiction, Ada was the real deal. Yet, whilst his name remains famous worldwide, Ada's memory is still being salvaged from the wastelands of the Arctic.

Ada was an Inuit from Alaska but because she was sent to a Methodist school at the age of 8, she never learnt crucial skills from the Inuits, such as fishing, shooting and building shelter in freezing conditions. All skills she would desperately need after being marooned on Wrangel, a desolate ice island north of Siberia.

Ada had married at 16 but her husband Jack Blackjack was abusive, starved and beat her. After two of her children died, she finally found the strength to leave him, taking her little boy Bennett with her. Unfortunately Bennet contracted tuberculosis, which was rife in Alaska at the time and required expensive treatment. Ada was broke and work was hard to find. She had to place her son in an orphanage whilst she struggled to raise money.

When she discovered a team of explorers were looking for native Inuit to accompany them on an Arctic expedition, although she was terrified of polar bears and guns, both in ample supply on this trip, the money offered was too good to refuse.

The expedition was organised by Vilhjalmur Stefansson, a famous and charming explorer, although he claimed the Arctic could be just as lovely to live in as Hawaii and all you needed was some common sense. (A patently ridiculous sentiment that would come back and frostbite him on the bum.)

Stefansson believed that Wrangel was habitable and would make a great air base for planes en route across the Arctic. Never mind that the Russians had already claimed Wrangel and that Stefansson himself had never been there. (Cue: *Mission Impossible* theme tune.)

However, Stefansson was very convincing and the men set out on their adventure buoyant and enthusiastic. They included the nominal leader Allan Crawford. Second-in-command was the big, burly Lorne Knight, followed by the unassuming Fred Maurer. Their assistant Milton Gale was only 19. Finally there was Ada, whose skills as a seamstress were vital to people living off the frozen lands.

Only two of those going had any experience, for the rest it would be a virgin trip. To add to this folly, the men only took enough supplies for six months, believing Stefansson's declaration that they would easily find food in the icy wilds. The most sensible advice Stefansson gave was to buy an umiak, a special boat that could be navigated through the frozen waters. This recommendation was ignored by the men, who decided the umiak was not worth the extortionate cost. They bought a tiny boat instead which was lost at sea after a vicious storm on the way to Wrangel.

They arrived in the summer season when there was plenty of game. However, as the winter set in, the animals became scarce and Wrangel became hell frozen over. The expedition cat Vic was the only one that didn't go hungry. Finally Crawford and Knight set out on a dangerous journey to get help. The treacherous conditions had them beat and they returned a couple of weeks later. By now Knight was suffering from scurvy. Leaving Ada behind with a very ill Knight, the men set off again in a different direction to seek assistance. They would never be seen again.

It was a massive shock for Ada to discover how desperately ill Lorne was and the realisation she would have to fend for them alone. She refused to give in and braving the elements taught herself how to trap properly (the men's traps had always failed) and conquered her fear of guns. When Lorne died in June, she only had the feline Vic for company. She was so lonely that she would sit beside Knight's corpse and talk to him. She was determined to stay alive and was finally rescued by a supply ship that came a few months later. She and the cat were the only survivors from the original party.

It had been an expedition of madness.

Agent 355

Say it enough times and it's just as catchy as 007. Except this renegade, a woman during the American Revolution, was effectively the USA's first female spy.

Agent 355 was the only woman in the six-member Culper Ring, a spy network created by US Major Benjamin Tallmadge on the orders of President Washington in 1778. This was during the British occupation of New York City and the Culper Ring would play a massive part in helping the Americans win their independence.

We're talking invisible ink and secret codes. In non-spy speak, the number 355 simply meant 'female spy'. They weren't called patriots in petticoats for nothing. If a female spy wore a black petticoat, it meant she had valuable information. White handkerchiefs referred to a safe rendezvous to exchange that info. And red petticoats meant a letter from Washington himself had arrived.

FYI, '711' referred to George Washington. (We'll let you try and work out the rationale.)

Agent 355, or 'The Lady', could have referred to any number of women working in New York City who were helping with information. Was she a specific person? Was she, as some suggest, Anna Smith Strong (also known as Nancy), whose husband Selah was captured and imprisoned on the notorious prison ship *Jersey*? Left to manage her family and New York farm alone, it's highly possible she worked for the Revolutionary cause and used her laundry line to send out covert information. (In honour of the famous general one of her sons was even named George Washington.)

Was she Elizabeth Burgin, known by many revolutionaries as a true heroine for delivering letters and helping an alleged 200 prisoners of war escape the clutches of the British? Although the majority of her actions are still shrouded in mystery, they were enough to ensure that Congress awarded her an annual pension.

Was she Sarah Horton Townsend, a cousin of Quaker Robert Townsend (code name Culper Jr, and known as 723) who was in charge of the Culper network? Or Sally Townsend, one of Robert's sisters? Their home, Raynham Hall in New York's Oyster Bay, was taken over by British officers when they captured Long Island. Sally fell in love with Lieutenant Colonel John Graves Simcoe – but on discovering vital information, did she betray him for the Revolutionary cause? Then there's Lydia Barrington Darragh, who managed to alert Washington to an impending attack on his troops.

Underestimating women being the norm, men on both sides of the American Revolution, whether Loyalist or Revolutionary, would have found it hard to countenance that their gentle, home-making, matronly women were involved in espionage. A perfect cover, then. If they had been caught, they would have been executed, no questions asked.

Whoever she was, she was damned good at her job and clearly had access to the upper echelons of British political and military society. In a massive coup for espionage, 355 helped expose Benedict Arnold and Major John Andre, the men in charge of England's intelligence operations in the Big Apple, who were fully prepared to betray their American side for the British.

Often referred to as the hidden daughter of the American Revolution, it is fair to say that General George Washington owed 355 a great deal.

Agostina Domenech
(4 March 1786–29 May 1857)

Also known as Augustina, Maid of Saragossa and the Spanish Joan of Arc, she was an ordinary woman who became a guerrilla fighter, warrior and heroine, immortalised in art by Francisco de Goya in his etchings *Disasters of War* and included in Lord Byron's poem *Childe Harold's Pilgrimage*.

It's thought Agostina was born in Reus, Tarragona, her family later moving to Madrid. She married young and had a son known only as Eugenio.

The Spanish royal family were prisoners of Bonaparte, who had installed his brother Joseph as de facto leader. Furious, the Spanish rose up in revolt during the Peninsular War (1807–14). The Spanish army was led by General José de Palafox.

Agostina was part of a larger women's resistance unit led by young noblewoman Countess Burita. In the summer of 1808 the unit defended the previously peaceful northern Spanish city of Zaragoza, part of Aragon, when it was attacked by Napoleon's army. Agostina helped the resistance by supplying the exhausted Spanish soldiers on the rampart walls with apples and water.

Terrified of the overwhelming odds stacked against them, and completely unprepared for a battle with the more experienced French, the Spanish abandoned their posts. Agostina, however, in scenes likely reminiscent of an *Expendables* movie, was made of stronger stuff.

Legend suggests that her lover was in charge of one of the cannon and was killed, leaving it unmanned. Hastily reloading the cannon and relighting the fuse from her dead paramour's hand, she let rip with a '26-pounder', literally in the faces of the group of oncoming French fighters. We're talking about a cannon that would normally need a team of men to operate it. And she did it by herself. The French were obliterated. General Palafox is quoted as saying he witnessed the event himself.

Blown away (not literally) by her outstanding bravery, the Spanish returned to their posts and together with Agostina carried on the fight for several weeks. The French were forced to temporarily lift their siege of the city. They came back later in the year, storming through the city, house by house, and resumed the devastating siege, where it's estimated that between 40,000 and 50,000 people died. In the midst of the fighting, Agostina was captured, only to escape later (see *Expendables II*).

As a female fighter, she may have been rare, but, in the words of John Lawrence Tone, 'women's resistance – through taking part in public demonstrations and revolts, stealing goods and weapons to supply the Spanish troops, and providing channels of communication and information to the guerilla groups – played a vital role in the Spanish defeat of Napoleon'. Later on she was made an actual officer in the Spanish army and is described as a guerrilla fighter, receiving a state pension and army medals for her efforts.

Anne of Cleves
(22 September 1515–16 July 1557)

In case you can't remember which of Henry VIII's wives she was, you might have to count on your fingers, or use the old adage 'divorced, beheaded, died, divorced, beheaded, survived'. Here's a clue: Anne was Number Four. There's much more to the women in Henry's life than a popular rhyme or having their lives purpose summed up by its inclusion in a list.

The daughter of Duke Johann III (known as John the Peaceful) and Maria of Jülich-Berg, Anne was, like many noble women of her era, used on the marriage market for political expediency. Arguably Henry VIII's most successful queen, Anne of Cleves was married to him for only six months. We'd argue that she got the better end of the deal by being relieved of her royal duty so early on.

Interestingly, Anne has been widely dismissed by history as the ugly one who Harry got rid of; the one wife for whom the legendary lothario could not 'get it up' for; the conjugal failure. So repulsed by her was he that he furiously called for a divorce from the 'Flanders mare' (by the way, this phrase was only used to describe her decades after her death, by Bishop Gilbert Burnet).

We'd like to put things into perspective. Whilst her physical reality may not have lived up to the image of her depicted in Hans Holbein's famous portrait, we prefer to imagine Anne's thoughts when she first caught sight of Henry. Popularly regarded as one of the world's most handsome, virile men, by the time they met, Henry was a mess. He was obese with a supperating, oozing, smelly and ulcerated wound on his leg, inflicted while participating in a jousting event.

'I like her not! I like her not!' yelled poor, old, disappointed Henry on meeting her for the first time. Seen from a different perspective, his outburst could be viewed as that of a petulant child, whose attempts at surprising his bride-to-be with a kiss whilst dressed in disguise (as was the tradition) failed miserably; he gave Anne the shock of her life and she allegedly spouted off a slew of German curses at him before realising who he was. It seemed the Flanders way of doing things was not up to scratch and the 24-year-old was simply not sophisticated enough for the Tudor court.

Their marriage was not consummated. Rather conveniently, Henry's spin doctors would have it that Anne's hideous features rendered him impotent. The real reason probably had more to do with the aforementioned huge girth and stinking, ulcerated leg. All this was moot as by 1540 Henry was head over heels (an unfortunate turn of phrase considering her eventual fate) with Anne's lady-in-waiting Catherine Howard.

Sophistication or not, Anne kept a level head on her shoulders (pun intended) and outlived not just her ex-husband, but all of Henry's other wives. She was clever and knew how to survive. She didn't put up a fight against the annulment and made everything easy for Henry, helping clear the way for his next marriage, a matter of weeks after the papers were signed.

She also arguably did better in the divorce than Henry did, awarded extensive property (including Hever Castle, Anne Boleyn's former home, showing Henry's propensity for neatly recycling property as well as wives), a generous income for life, jewels and the good favour of the king, who would hereafter refer to her as 'sister'. The divorce made her one of the wealthiest women in England (nice work if you can get it). Most importantly, she lived, which is more than can be said of Thomas Cromwell (who pushed for the marriage) and Catherine Howard, his fifth wife, who were both put to death.

She is buried in Westminster Abbey, the only one of Henry's wives to be afforded the honour.

Aspasia of Miletus
(*c.* 470–*c.* 400 BC)

Information on individual Greek women is in short supply, making the fact that we do know something of Aspasia all the more remarkable. Described as one of the most famous women of Athens, her name, which may not have been her real one, variously means 'welcome', 'embrace' or 'desired one'. But she is still only remembered for being the mistress of Pericles, the great statesman and politician from Athens, and through the opinions (good, bad and downright ugly) of the many Greek writers and poets of the day who spoke of her.

Born in Miletus (in modern-day Turkey), Aspasia's family were wealthy enough for her to benefit from a fantastic education, better than the average Greek woman. Depending on whose viewpoint you take, on emigrating to Athens in around 450 BC, she was either a brothel keeper, *hetaira* (prostitute who offered companionship and educated conversation, similar to a courtesan) or ran an intellectual salon for the great and good men of Greece. A *hetaira* would be conversant in topics ranging from science, literature and art to history, politics and philosophy.

A contemporary and friend of Socrates, she's mentioned by Plato and also in the writings of Plutarch, Aristophanes and Xenophen, suggesting that she was well-known and respected. She's also cited in the *Encyclopaedia Britannica* of the day, the tenth-century Byzantine *Suda*, and described as 'clever with regards to words', and was a philosophy and rhetoric teacher.

She and Pericles, who divorced his wife for her, had a son together by 440 BC, also called Pericles. Whether they ever married is unclear, although it is doubtful because she was a '*metic*', or immigrant, as opposed to a 'real' Athenian citizen, and the laws of the land would have prohibited their union. Ironically, because of her immigrant status, she wasn't bound by the usual restrictions applied to Greek women; she had much more freedom.

Regardless of the rules and in direct opposition to how Greek men were meant to treat their wives or partners, Pericles was open in his admiration and adoration of Aspasia. Apparently, people were appalled that he publicly kissed her goodbye before he went to work and on his return home. He received a lot of criticism for this from Greek writers and poets of the day, whilst she was viciously slandered ('whore' or 'dog-eyed concubine') because of her unseemly influence on him.

Although satirist Lucian of Samosata called her a 'model of wisdom', Aspasia faced fierce disapproval from the women of Athens, who accused her of corrupting the women of their city to satisfy the sexual perversions of her partner Pericles. After he died she went on to have an affair with Pericles's friend Lysicles; after his death, she disappears from history.

Aud/Unn or Audunn the Deep-minded (AD 834–900)

The ninth century was a busy time for Norwegians, with many deciding to emigrate and trade with their neighbours. With last names like Skull-Splitter and Blood-Axe, which leave little to the imagination, they also did a lot of raiding and had rather complicated lines of family, alliances and lineage. They are also credited with bestowing on us the traditional Icelandic Sagas, some of the world's most incredible and significant poetry, and were legendary explorers, storytellers and artists.

Aud was the daughter of Norwegian Viking chieftain Ketil Flatnose and his wife Ketil and the wife of Olaf the White, the Viking King of Dublin. Her gods were Odin, Thor and Freya. Thanks to her wealth (she's also known as Aud the Deep-Wealthy) and high rank, as a woman Aud had considerable freedom (relative to her fellow women across the rest of the world).

After being widowed, she helped her son Thorstein the Red conquer half of Scotland before he was killed in battle, after which Aud took a good look at her future prospects in Scotland and realised they were bleak. She had a huge Viking merchant ship, or knarr, made in secret from wood in nearby forests. Then she got the rest of her family together, threw in some Scottish and Irish slaves and 'got the hell out of Dodge', decamping to a largely unexplored Iceland. Upon arrival, she gave the slaves their freedom and land. Let's not underestimate the enormity of what they faced on their journey in an open boat, crammed with people, livestock and the rest of their household. Consolidating her dynasty, she married off two of her granddaughters on the way, during stops at the Faroe Islands and the Orkneys.

In spite of a frosty Icelandic welcome from her brother, she claimed vast amounts of land, settled down in Laxdale and was an early convert to Christianity. With the men in her life dead, she became a true Viking matriarch in Iceland; her exploits are famously recounted in the Laxdaela Saga.

Upon her death, she was given a no-expenses send-off to Valhalla and is the only recorded Viking woman to be honoured with a full Viking ship funeral.

Audrey Hepburn
(4 May 1929–20 January 1993)

In a world obsessed with image and celebrity, pictures of glamorous Audrey Hepburn from the Hollywood era still decorate our walls in boxed IKEA frames.

Whilst it's almost impossible to talk about her without referencing her iconic beauty, it was something she was not concerned with. It must have shocked Hollywood to the core that she cared not a jot about ageing. She could have been a personality reduced to mass-produced merchandise reminiscent of Hollywood's Golden Age, but thankfully her humanitarian work with UNICEF has helped give us a more balanced, three-dimensional perspective on this amazing woman, member of the Dutch Resistance and human rights campaigner. This is one film icon who possessed even more star quality in her private life than on screen.

Audrey lived under the terrifying Nazi occupation of Holland in the town of Arnhem, which witnessed excessive cruelty, battles between the Germans and the British, as well as starvation and deprivation. Her childhood story reads like one of *La La Land*'s better scripts, set against a dangerous background of Nazi occupation, involvement with the Dutch Resistance and secret ballet performances in blacked out rooms to silent applause.

From the age of 12 she, like many Dutch children, delivered notes hidden in her shoes to the Dutch Resistance. On one occasion she was late home from her tutor's house and in the precarious situation of being out beyond curfew. She must have felt absolute terror when she was stopped by a German soldier who demanded to see inside her shoes. By sheer luck that day she was not carrying her contraband and the soldier let her go home. She also escaped the Nazis when she was rounded up one day with other women. Spotting a chance to flee, she ran to hide in the cellar of a city council building.

This small Dutch town faced further trauma when the people suffered terrible starvation in the so-called 'Hunger Winter' of 1944. When UNICEF's forerunner the United Nations Relief and Rehabilitation Administration arrived to help, Audrey remembered clearly the first two things they gave her – cigarettes and condensed milk. This was the start of her lifelong journey with UNICEF helping the most impoverished children in the world.

A survivor of the war's atrocities, nightmares she carried to the end of her days, she channelled her energies into helping the most disadvantaged kids across the globe. She understood that as a famous actress she could draw much-needed publicity for terrible situations throughout the world. Travelling extensively for UNICEF, from Ethiopia to the Sudan to Bangladesh and many other distressed countries, she was a beacon of hope and comfort to the children she met.

Azucena Villaflor
(7 April 1924–10 December 1977)

This woman had guts. She was an ordinary wife and mother, until political circumstances forced her down an entirely different road; one where she would found a human rights movement against a corrupt dictatorship. It was a path that would ultimately lead to her own death, together with the other founding members of the Madres of the Desaparecidos (Disappeared) movement, or the Mothers of Plaza de Mayo.

After the military coup of 1976 overthrew President Isabel Perón, Argentina was run by a brutal dictatorship. This 'Dirty War' would last until 1983, and its leaders would be responsible for, amongst much other violence and bloodshed, the Falklands War.

One of Azucena's four sons, Nestor De Vicenti, was abducted with his fiancée Raquel Mangin a few months into this military junta. There was no word of explanation or support from the government. Nestor and Raquel, both 24 years old, had become members of the forcibly 'disappeared'. They would never be seen again.

Frustrated by the lack of information and desperately anxious for her son's safety, Azucena led other mothers, and grandmothers, in the same situation as her. From 1977 they would meet each Thursday at the Plaza de Mayo in Buenos Ares, directly opposite the main government building, the Casa Rosada. They would walk around the square in peaceful protest, demanding that the government give them information on their missing children and grandchildren, whose names were emblazoned on their white headscarves. Azucena would encourage, organise and mobilise the women.

On 10 December 1977, the same day that the Mothers had paid for a newspaper advertisement, demanding justice and featuring over 800 of their signatures together with the names of their missing children, Azucena was herself abducted from outside her home. The dictatorship saw her as a threat and wanted to send a powerful message to the other Mothers.

Her anonymous corpse was later discovered in the Río de la Plata, with four other bodies. But her remains, together with those of Esther Ballestrino de Careaga and Maria Eugenia Ponce de Bianco, and a nun who supported the Mothers, were only finally identified in 2005 by a special Argentinian forensics team, dedicated to discovering the truth of the fate of victims of the political purge. The women had been victims of so-called death flights; tortured, drugged and then thrown out of aeroplanes into the sea. It's estimated that up to 30,000 people were murdered in this way by the regime.

On 8 December 2005 the cremated remains of Azucena, Esther and Maria were interred at Plaza de Mayo. The protests there would continue until 2006, when many of the Mothers of the Desaparecidos were in their 80s.

In 2007, the country elected human-rights champion Cristina Fernández de Kirchner as its first female elected President. During her time in office she was passionate about bringing crimes during the Dirty War to justice. Azucena's, Esther's and Maria's deaths were not in vain. Their legacy was a public and determined fight for justice through human rights courts, the prosecution of the military leaders of the former dictatorship and proof of the power of peaceful protest. They know that their children are never coming back, but today the Mothers of Plaza de Mayo still demand answers to their fate.

Calamity Jane
(1 May 1852–1903)

Martha Jane Canary was no wallflower. Fiesty, reckless and with enough confidence to fill both barrels of her guns, the moniker 'Calamity Jane' grew from her reputation as one who could cause calamitous problems.

Jane however had a completely different take on how she acquired her nickname. She claimed it was after a particularly heroic act in 1872 when she rescued Captain Egan on Goose Creek in Wyoming whilst employed as a scout for General Custer. At great risk she rode to his rescue and carried him to safety after he was shot. Dramatically, he declared: 'I name you Calamity Jane: heroine of the plains.'

It's difficult to separate the truth from the exaggerations made by Martha Jane in her ghost-written autobiography and dime novels – stories that helped make her a buck or two – and by some of the less flattering accounts written about her. Add the sweet as apple pie version in the Doris Day musical and it's easy to forget that she was an alcoholic and probably a prostitute. She saw fit to airbrush these salient facts from her autobiography – a shame as her real story would have been so much more insightful had she written honestly about surviving the Wild West as a pioneer woman, orphaned at 14 with five younger siblings to care for, rather than giving us a stick'em'up cowboy show.

In those dark days Martha took every job going; dishwasher, dancer, ox-driver and, perhaps at one point, prostitution. How easy would it have been for a teenage girl left alone with dependents to survive during those harsh settler times? Those days are a testament to her extraordinary character. Sadly she was more interested in recounting how well she shot, rode and fought. Sitting in our hard-won feminist armchairs of the twenty-first century, can we really blame her? It was the men's daring tales that sold papers and she needed money. In June of 1876 she claimed that she worked as a pony express rider, a dangerous occupation that attracted ruthless bandits. But she tells us that such fiends left her alone, fearful of her reputation as a crack shot.

She also waxed lyrical about her days as a scout in General Custer's army in 1870 and 1871, where she donned the clothes of her fellow soldiers. Of course riding out to fight in hoops and bustles would have been a feat too far even for the irrepressible Jane. However, Captain Jack Crawford, an active scout and soldier during the campaigns Jane apparently fought in, wrote an article contesting all her claims. He lambasted the press for their sensationalism and categorical fiction written as newspaper articles. Patronisingly he praised her for her generosity and said she could have been a great wife and mother if she had not been forced to scrabble for survival after her parents's death. He then goes on to discredit every story written by or about her, discounting her as a scout, mail carrier, stage drive and friend of Bill Hickock.

Yet Calamity was reputed by many sources to have been very kind, something she was weirdly modest about considering all her other wild boasts. She is particularly remembered for nursing smallpox victims, an act every bit as plucky as her intrepid fights but considered a woman's duty not a courageous deed. But these stories wouldn't have earned the same dollars and dimes as her 'Injun' battles'. Nor were they the actions people wanted to see when she later performed in *Buffalo Bill's Wild West* show, where she showed off her shooting and equestrian skills in 1895, or whilst travelling with a dime-museum show.

Whilst much has been written about her life as a frontierswoman and her heroics with the Native Americans it seems we know as little about her as we do about other forgotten women in history. Did she even meet, never mind marry, Wild Bill Hickock? Did he even know her? Was she really buried next to him as a joke because he said she was annoying? Did she fearlessly ride out to battle and deliver vital information? Did she have a daughter? What everyone seems to agree on is that her life is too shrouded in legend and exaggeration to ever properly know the truth. Martha, aka Jane, was clearly a master storyteller and performer, not to mention a survivor and adventurer – not the worst legacy to leave behind.

Cartimandua
(*c.* AD 43–*c.* 70)

When the Romans invaded Britain they encountered two queens from different tribes, the Iceni and the Brigantia. These queens were contemporaries but whilst Boudicca is well known, Cartimandua is not. They are both described as women warriors – so why was only Boudicca a major player in history?

Boudicca fulfilled an image of the romantic rebel defending her culture against the dastardly Roman invasion, whereas Cartimandua decided to take a more pragmatic approach of appeasement. In a system known as client monarchy Cartimandua swore loyalty to Rome and in return retained autonomy of her realm.

A northern lass hailing from what would become James Herriot's bright and beautiful Yorkshire, Cartimandua was the queen of the Brigantes, considered by the Romans to be the largest tribe in Britain. Most of our knowledge comes from the Roman historian Tacitus, a misogynist who was most assuredly politically and gender biased (see Messalina for more of his chauvinistic nonsense). He was especially censorious of women who were disloyal and committed adultery. In his eyes Cartimandua was both an adulteress and a traitor. However, loyalty is in the eye of the beholder and her eyes saw a series of revolts led by her own ex-husband to claim her throne. (Exes – pah! Nothing but trouble.)

She is most maligned for having delivered Caratacus, leader of the Catuvellauni tribe, in chains to the Romans in AD 51. His rebellion in Wales had failed and he fled to her for shelter. Britain was a patchwork quilt of different tribes and they were not all united. Cartimandua may have considered him just as much a rival as the Romans but it was the Romans she had sworn fealty to.

Perhaps Caratacus hoped her Roman-hating husband Valentius would aid him. Alas, Cartimandua held the power, Valentius was merely her consort. Does this really make her a traitor? Tacitus was never one for letting facts get in the way of a good story. Certainly it worked well for her strategically as she was rewarded handsomely and received critical Roman support during the insurrections that followed.

Cartimandua and her husband Valentius were not a happy couple. Whether they married for love or political reasons, they were the couple that always caused a scene. However, their scenes provoked civil wars. During one vicious marital spat, aka revolt, Cartimandua captured some of her in-laws (well you would, wouldn't you?). Valentius, however, had a great deal of support from Brigantes who were fed up of kow-towing to Rome. Valentius went full throttle and was only subdued after the Roman cavalry marched to Cartimandua's aid.

If the marriage had been on its last legs before, these legs had been amputated. To compound Velantius' antipathy towards her, Cartimandua decided to divorce him in favour of his arms bearer. A furious Valentius started plotting another coup, building support and biding his time for revenge.

That time came in AD 69 when Emperor Nero died, leaving Rome in dire straits with a dangerous power vacuum. Valentius saw his chance and struck again. This time the Romans could only spare a few men to help Cartimandua and barely escaping with her life, she fled to Deva, a Roman stronghold in what is nowadays Chester.

Valentius was King of the Yorkshire hills for all of 2 seconds before the Romans decided he was a pest and took over the Brigantes once and for all.

As for Cartimandua, her name never appears again in any records. What happened to her and where did she go? It would seem that after seeking a haven with the Romans, her role was now entirely inconsequential to them or perhaps she went into witness protection and eked out her days as Claudia the Vestal Virgin.

Catherine the Great
(2 May 1729–17 November 1796)

Catherine II of Russia wasn't Russian. And her name wasn't even Catherine.

Russia's longest reigning female leader was actually born in Prussia as Sophie von Anhalt-Zerbst, daughter of the poor and little known Prussian prince Christian August von Anhalt-Zerbst. Her mother, Princess Johanna Elisabeth of Holstein-Gottorp, had grand designs for her daughter's future as well as her own social standing. She used her connections with nobility to push them both up the royal ladder.

The ruler of Russia at that time was Peter the Great's daughter, Empress Elizabeth. Unmarried and without children, she'd appointed her nephew Peter as heir and was on the hunt for a suitable wife for him. In 1744, Sophie was invited to the Russian court at St Petersburg.

In 1745, she would marry her cousin, grandson of the legendary Peter the Great and heir to the Russian Romanov throne, more commonly known as

Grand Duke Peter. He would become Peter III in 1761 and, quite frankly, was not accomplished at kingship. To say the newlyweds didn't like each other would be a masterpiece in understatement. There would be no children for eight years.

Both husband and wife embarked on affairs and Catherine, amongst her many paramours, would have a famed relationship with Gregory Potemkin. Being involved with Catherine was often a great career move; she used her influence to get one lover on the Polish throne as king, although later she'd change her mind and get him to abdicate. With all the bed-hopping going on, the legitimacy of their son Paul, eventually born in 1754, is highly questionable.

Peter III couldn't rule to save his life. Ironic, considering that Sophie, now Grand Duchess Catherine Alekseyevna, was soon involved in a plot with her lover of the hour, military officer Grigory Orlov, to overthrow him. With the support of the military, she would be pronounced Empress of Russia in July 1762 whilst her husband would be arrested, forced to abdicate and bumped off by Orlov's brother. Gotta love Russian politics.

What would follow next? Affairs, murder, political intrigue, revolting Cossacks and peasants. Catherine would rule until her death in 1796. A passionate patron of the arts, Catherine used some of her personal collection to launch the sumptuous Hermitage Museum, was pen pals with Voltaire and extended Russian territory through a series of successful wars (including one against the entire Ottoman Empire), adding Crimea and much of Poland and the Ukraine to it. She began the process of westernising Russia, founded schools; for girls and introduced a bank which offered the first paper money in Russia. She was a tremendous advocate for reform.

She died on 17 November 1796, most likely from a stroke and not, as her political detractors would have you believe, engaged in flagrante with a horse. Or relieving herself on the toilet.

Ching Shih
(1775–1844)

Ching Shih is notorious for transitioning from a prostitute to a powerful pirate queen, commanding around 80,000 men and almost 2,000 ships. She held the South China Sea in thrall, terrorising China, England and Portugal's armadas.

Ching first enters historical consciousness whilst working as a prostitute on Canton's flower boats, a euphemism for floating brothels. The boats were described as ornate and lush, housing several prostitutes and used to host grand parties. The Chinese population would not allow prostitution on shore in case this contaminated the land. Clearly it was perfectly okay to let pimp boats contaminate the waters.

Where did Ching Shih come from? How did she end up as a sex worker on board these watery brothels? And what on earth was her name because Ching Shih translates as Cheng's widow and is a label, not a birth-given name? Such is the frustration of writing about women for whom no real records exist and certainly nothing was written by them in person. We can only speculate.

Some historians believe Ching Shih was a big deal on her flower boat, with access to China's coterie of powerful VIPs, privy to their secrets and able to manipulate them. For that reason the Pirate Lord Cheng I, commander of the infamous Red Flag Fleet of Pirates, asked her to marry him. It would be a successful business arrangement that provided him with her vital inside knowledge as well as a brilliant strategist by his side.

Ching Shih demanded equal control as her dowry. The two of them ran the pirate trade like the 'Sopranos of the Sea', capturing men from the armadas to join them and using fear, intimidation and downright greed to tempt rival pirate gangs. Apparently these men were offered the choice beween being nailed to the deck and beaten to death or joining the Red gang. Tough decision.

We don't know the exact nature of their marriage. Cheng's sexual tastes seemed to run towards a young fisherman he'd captured called Cheung Po; clearly his favourite, in a bizarre twist that may upset twenty-first-century delicate sensitivities, Cheng adopted him, making him both a son and lover. This was purely a shrewd business move that allowed him to name Cheung as his heir.

When Cheng met his untimely end, either as the victim of a tornado or murdered in Vietnam – sources disagree – you might expect Ching Shih, having outlived her usefulness as Cheng's appendage, to fade into obscurity. But one does not survive the dangerous world of Canton's prostitution rings without learning something about survival. Before Cheng's body was cold in the ground, Ching seduced Cheung Po and married him – a puppet husband giving her the authority to bring the Red Fleet pirates to her shapely heel.

Her reign of crime and punishment was a paradoxical mix. On the one hand, British prisoner Richard Glasspoole said they were a structured, disciplined yet brutally ruthless organisation. According to Mr Glasspoole, their raids were savage and punishments for dissent merciless. However the code of conduct that Ching Shih insisted on was enlightened. Rape was punishable by death, including rape of female captives. If the pirates wanted to sleep with a woman they had to marry her and stay faithful. So you could pillage but not rape.

When the Chinese army became too threatening, Ching Shih eventually negotiated inspired terms of surrender, which allowed her to retire rich and, crucially, alive.

Christina of Sweden
(18 December 1626–19 April 1689)

Christina refused to conform. She did things her way, with little regard for anyone else. Her parents expected a boy and her mother was devastated when her birth – she emerged covered in dark hair – proved otherwise. 'Instead of a son, I am given a daughter, dark and ugly, with a great nose and black eyes. Take her from me, I will not have such a monster!'

Christina's father however was adamant that a little thing like gender wasn't going to get in the way of him raising a prince. Christina attended council meetings from the age of 14. 'It is said the queen actually tried to injure her child, and throughout Christina's early childhood there were a number of odd accidents: the child was dropped head first on the floor, permanently injuring her shoulder; a beam fell over the cradle; little Christina tumbled down stairs.'

Following the death of her father King Gustav II Adolph in battle (his wife Maria Eleanora of Brandenburg went completely bonkers with grief, kept his heart a casket swinging above her bed, and only allowed the king to be buried nineteen months after his untimely end), Christina assumed the Swedish throne. Her mother Maria, known for her mental instability and episodes of acute hysteria, was soon cast aside.

Christina was a true intellectual, studied with French philosopher Descartes, was extravagant, an avid art patron and is thought to have had a passionate lesbian relationship with her lady-in-waiting Countess Ebba Sparre, with whom she shared a bed (although that was fairly common practice at the time). She was also was rumoured to have been a hermaphrodite. She cut her hair short, wore men's clothes, swore like a trooper, had a deep masculine voice and her table manners would have made a Viking blush.

But on 6 June 1654, when she was 27 and after two years of negotiations with her council, Christina abdicated her throne in favour of her cousin Carl, with home she had a brief, secret engagement. She never married or had children. To the shock of her nation, she converted to Roman Catholicism, a criminal offence in Lutheran Sweden, moved to the Farnese Palace at the Vatican to continue her intellectual pursuits and established a well-known cultural salon.

Despite the fact she'd abdicated, she seemed confused about what she could and couldn't do. She had courtier the Marquis of Mondaleschia brutally murdered in front of her for ruining her attempts to become Queen of Naples by betraying her plans. She also failed in her own attempt to become Queen of Poland.

Christina died in 1689 at the age of 63 and is buried in St Peter's in the Vatican (a rare honour for anyone, let alone a mere woman).

Cixi
(29 November 1835–15 November 1908)

The Dragon Empress began life as a girl from Beijing named Yehenara, the daughter of middle-ranking Manchu officials.

The last Empress of the Chinese Qing Dynasty started her political and court life as a 16-year-old third-class concubine in the harem of the Emperor Xianfeng. Her brains, intellect and, as legend has it, beautiful singing voice brought her to his attention. Her name was added to his list of nightly bedfellows and eunuchs would deliver her, naked, to the foot of his bed.

Giving birth to a son soon helped boost her kudos in the eyes of the court; the emperor named her Tzu Hsi (modern spelling Cixi), 'empress of the western palace'. In a sign of things to come, she began helping the emperor, as she could read and write Chinese and offering up her opinions on state affairs. Clearly aware of what trouble her interference could cause, the emperor appointed a regency of eight men to rule China after his death.

After that event in 1861, a completely unfazed Cixi teamed up with Empress Zhen, Xianfeng's official widow. Thanks to some truly mind-blowing political shenanigans, plotting and the ruthless 'suicide' of two of the regents, she elevated her own 5-year-old son to dizzy new heights as the new Emperor Tongzhi.

The promotion made her Empress Dowager and de facto regent, the power 'behind the curtains' (chui lian ting zheng), a position she kept until stepping down when her son, by then an alcoholic, turned 17. Eventually she turned her attentions elsewhere, spending huge amounts of government money on a new Summer Palace.

However when Tongzhi. died two years later from smallpox and venereal disease, she became regent once more for her 3-year-old nephew Guangxu, neatly side-stepping the potential ascendancy of Tongzhi's wife, Cixi's own daughter-in-law, who was pregnant with their child. Both conveniently 'died'.

Cixi 'retired' in 1889 but came back very quickly when China was defeated by Japan in the first Sino-Japanese War. She ruthlessly tried to turn back the clock on reforms her nephew had implemented, executing anyone who got in her way.

Her reign was a disaster for China. She encouraged the instigators of the Boxer Rebellion uprising (citizens in northern China opposed to what they regarded as the disastrous, modernising effect of the West) and its siege of an area where foreign missionaries and merchants lived. A huge number of them died before armies of the West captured Peking and put an end to the violence. After governing, directly or indirectly for fifty years, she suffered a stroke in 1907. She was still compos mentis enough to appoint her grandnephew Pu Yi as Emperor of China, but he would be the last.

Was she as ruthless and bloodthirsty in her ambition as history tells us – or was she guilty simply by virtue of being a woman acting as a man would? Her final resting place was robbed by revolutionaries in 1928 but restored by the People's Republic of China in 1949.

Cleopatra
(*c.* 69 BC–12 August 30 BC)

Politically astute, multi-lingual, intelligent, ambitious and tenacious, Cleopatra VII Philopator was the last of the Egyptian Pharoahs, the last of the Ptolemy Dynasty that had been established by Alexander the Great.

She was on the throne from 51 BC until her death in 30 BC and noted for being a powerful and unifying female ruler at a time dominated by men. Many historians believe she was actually Greek by birth. She also had a goddess-complex, believing herself to be the reincarnation of Egyptian goddess Isis.

She was renowned (obviously, see 'complex', above) for her dramatic entrances and exits – whether being lowered majestically into a bath of ass's milk, smuggled into see Julius Caesar via a carpet or committing suicide, allegedly via the poisonous bite of an asp. About that asp. Cleopatra's well-known suicide is about as authentic as a politician's platitudes. Cleopatra knew her poisons well (one must, after all, have fun with one's condemned prisoners). She would have known that an asp bite is phenomenally painful and might not have even proved fatal. It's more likely she created a delicious cocktail using less painful ingredients such as opium and wolf's bane. But of course there is no good story without its counter conspiracy theory. The 'Moulder-Scully' brigade suspect poor Cleo was bumped off by political enemies.

Married to her 10-year-old brother Ptolemy XIII, as was custom, 17- or 18-year-old Cleopatra became co-regent in Alexandria when her father Ptolemy XII died. As per that custom, it's also likely that Cleopatra's mother was her father's sister: her own aunt. Sent into exile after she tried to seize power for herself, Cleo fled to Syria to gather an army. Julius Caesar, meanwhile, came to the palace in 48 BC from the more powerful Rome. He wanted to hold a peace conference between the two siblings, after all, a peaceful Alexandria was in Rome's best interests.

Banned by Ptolemy from re-entering her own city, Cleopatra smuggled herself in, via a carpet (or as has been suggested, a clothing sack), to ask for the general's help. The dramatic performance worked. Her brother's forces were defeated at the subsequent Battle of Nile and Ptolemy himself drowned. Cleopatra moved to Rome with Caesar and had his son, Caesarion, although he refused to acknowledge him as his own.

The short, short version of what ensued: it's 44 BC and Caesar is assassinated ('Et tu Brute?'); Cleopatra returns to Egypt, marries her other brother, Ptolemy XIV, then murders him soon after to protect Caesarion's political future and then she assassinates her pesky sister Arsinoe. Still with us?

In 41 BC Cleopatra falls in love with Marc Anthony and they form a romantic and political alliance, the latter against Roman leader Octavian Caesar. The two lovebirds are defeated by the aforementioned Caesar (Boo! Hiss!) at the Battle of Actium and both commit suicide, although not at the same time, because that would have been far too messy. (Cue: Elizabeth Taylor, Richard Burton and a box of Kleenex). Their three children, Ptolemy Philadelphus and the twins Cleopatra Selene and Alexander Helios, are taken to Rome to be raised by Marc Anthony's widow Octavia.

Don't let Hollywood fool you; Cleo's death wasn't a romantic one. It wasn't an act of heartbroken despair at the death of her beloved Marc Anthony, but instead a calculated move to preserve her dignity. If she had been captured by Octavian (the first Emperor of Rome, who renamed himself Augustus, in honour of the month of August marking Cleopatra's death) he would have paraded her as a trophy of war through the streets of Rome.

No way was she going to give Caesar the last word in the Empire's war of propaganda. In life, as in death, Cleopatra had control of her image. Exit: stage left.

Coco Chanel
(19 August 1883–10 January 1971)

On behalf of every woman who has ever received an invite to a posh do and thought 'What on earth do do I wear', we wish to thank Mademoiselle Coco Chanel from the top of our heads all the way down to the hem of our little black dress. Without her revolutionary talent and exquisite eye for detail, this design masterpiece would never have graced wardrobes everywhere. Prior to Chanel's elegant design in 1912, black was only worn by mourners, but women took up the idea with more excited fervour than a hoard of shopaholics on Black Friday.

Sartorially speaking, Coco, actually christened Gabrielle, enhanced the world of fashion. She may not have been the first to embrace the practical and sporty 'garçonne' look (a woman with short hair and short dresses) but her designs became the ultimate must-have, helping women everywhere to burst free from corsets and shake bustles off their booty into clothes they could actually breathe in.

It could be said that those clothes were only liberating to those women who had a flat-chested coat-hanger body, rather like Chanel herself. Boobs were not de rigueur and so these fashions must have been an exercise in self-loathing for those more graciously endowed. She hated the lumps and bumps that ruined the line of her creations and abhorred those of us who were plus grosse.

Unfortunately boobs, tums and bums were not the only object of her vitriol. At the age of 12 her mother died and her errant father placed her and her sisters in a strict Catholic convent in Auberge. It's possible that amid the harsh disciplinarian routine of the convent, little Coco was fully indoctrinated into the popular anti-Semitic beliefs of the day, including the favourite accusation that the Jews killed Jesus Christ. She was rabidly anti-Semitic but would put it aside for a lucrative business deal such as the development of the Chanel No. 5 brand with the very Jewish Wertheimer brothers.

She never trusted them though, and the business relationship was fraught with legal battles over ownership and rights. When Nazi Germany started taking businesses away from Jews, she clapped her manicured hands in glee waiting to do the same in France. The Wertheimers were nobody's fool and had placed the perfume business in the proxy hands of a Gentile (non-Jew) much earlier before fleeing to the US to wait out the war.

Luckily she was consoled by her Aryan Adonis Baron Hans Gunther von Dincklage, who charmed his way into persuading elite and influential Europeans to turn informants for the Nazis. The big question was how far did Coco go in her support for the Nazis? According to H. Vaughn, she was definitely a spy charged with running Operation Westminster, an alternative peace deal with Churchill for the SS officers who had lost faith in Hitler.

She was certainly a nasty opportunist and enjoyed a lavish party lifestyle during the war in the Ritz where she hobnobbed happily with SS elite. But she could switch her allegiances as fast as her customers changed their handbags. At the end of the war she rushed to give out bottles of her perfume to the American GIs returning home. A show of Allied loyalty or an inspired PR move? She may have been unpleasant but she was an incredibly gifted designer and astute businesswoman who lived the ultimate rags-to-riches story.

Edith Cavell
(4 December 1865–12 October 1915)

An incredibly brave and patriotic First World War British nurse who believed unequivocally in her vocation and her duty to God, Edith was blindfolded and shot for treason by a German firing squad in 1915.

Born in Swardeston, a village near Norwich, to Anglican priest the Reverend Frederick Cavell and his young wife Louisa, Edith embraced her schooling in Kensington, Clevedon and Peterborough, where she learned French. Then came a period of working as a governess, before she decided to broaden her horizons and travel to Austria and Bavaria, where she donated some of her inherited money to a hospital. Returning home to look after her ailing father was a pivotal moment; she decided to pursue nursing and undertook gruelling training at the London Hospital in 1896.

A year later, she was awarded the Maidstone Medal for her work in saving lives during the summer typhoid outbreak in Maidstone in 1897; only 132 died out of the 1,700 infected. She then spent time nursing for private clients as well as at St Pancras Infirmary and Shoreditch Infirmary (where she launched the novel idea of follow-up visits for patients who had been discharged) before becoming Matron at Salford Sick Poor and Private Nursing Institution.

In September 1907, her reputation having preceded her, Belgian royal surgeon Dr Antoine Depage (whose wife would perish on the RMS *Lusitania*) invited her to run L'École Belge d'Infirmières Diplômées, the first Belgian medical school, based in his Berkendael Institute. Just five years later, she had made her mark; her qualified nurses were much sought after by hospitals and schools, and in 1913 by Queen Elisabeth of Belgium, herself a close friend of Depage, when she broke her arm.

When war broke out, though she was visiting her mother in Britain, she insisted on returning to her work in Brussels. Soon after military action began, Austrian, British, French and Belgian wounded came for treatment at her infirmary. To ensure it remained politically neutral, Edith turned it into a Red Cross hospital. (Depage was founder and president of the Belgian branch.)

Following the Battle of Mons on 23 August 1914, when many Allied soldiers were left trapped behind enemy lines, she hid around 200 of them there before helping them escape German-occupied Belgium into neutral Holland through a secret underground network run by architect Philippe Baucq.

Recent Belgian archived war material uncovered by Dame Stella Rimington, DCB and former Director-General of M15, shows that, contrary to public opinion at the time, the members of Edith's network weren't just acting as humanitarians; they were in fact providing covert espionage intelligence for the British. There is little doubt Cavell didn't have at least some inkling of what was going on.

Philippe Baucq was caught at the end of July 1915 and evidence was discovered that incriminated Edith. Arrested by the German secret police, after three days of questioning, her captors tricked her and told her that her fellow prisoners had confessed everything; if she confessed, she would save them. She believed them – and told them all she knew, condemning herself in the process.

Despite frantic American and Spanish diplomatic efforts to intervene, she was kept in solitary confinement before finally being shot by a firing squad in the early hours of 12 October, at the Tir National shooting range, alongside Philippe Baucq and three other Belgian nationals. She was buried in the prison grounds.

The Germans were stunned by the furious outpouring of censure from the international public and press at her murder, but it was great for the British war effort; voluntary sign-ups to the army massively increased as a direct result.

At the end of the war, her body was exhumed and a service attended by the King and Queen of Belgium was held in her honour. Her body was then transported with great dignity and ceremony back to England for a memorial ceremony attended by Queen Alexandra, the Queen Mother. She is now buried in her beloved Norwich, in the grounds of the cathedral. Today the Cavell Trust provides assistance to nurses in need.

Eliza Josolyne
(1833–1907)

Bedlam – that way madness lies. The very name makes most of us shudder, picturing images of people battered by its cruel practices and torturous 'cures', chained to filthy walls, their humanity stripped away. Bedlam was the stuff of nightmares particularly as it had a reputation for incarcerating perfectly sane people (mainly women) by corrupt doctors paid off by families that wanted rid. (So much easier than divorce.)

More terrifying were the many people committed for reasons of insanity that, quite frankly, we would consider insane, such as adultery, exhaustion, epilepsy and truly heinous behaviour such as flirting or talking back to your parents. An extreme solution to teenage aggravation.

The association of madness with women was so rife that it seems only right to address Bedlam. Inmate Eliza Josolyne's experience provides just one insight into this insane period of history.

She was brought to Bedlam after struggling to clean a house of at least twenty rooms by herself, which included the onerous task of lighting fires in each of the rooms every day. Whilst she could never be considered lucky, at least when Eliza Josolyne was admitted to Bethlem (the real name of Bedlam), the Victorians had had a change in attitude towards the mentally ill, treating them with more compassion. Bethlem was much improved since its earlier days – it couldn't have got much worse – although it was still far from a Californian retreat. Unfortunately Eliza would later be admitted to the incurables ward and live there until her death.

The popular image of the savage mad man had been replaced by the crazed, hysterical female, an idea well ingrained in the Victorian imagination, from trashy romance to literary greats such as Jane Eyre's woman in the attic. The overriding belief was that the mentally ill needed to be confined under the leadership of a strong patriarchial leader who would restore order to their minds. The brutality of the treatments depended on the patriarch in charge. Eliza, who had already had four spells in the institution for mania, would experience many of Bethlem's transformations, from the earlier medical Superintendent Hopkins' belief that restraints should be abolished to Dr Isaac Brown's view that restraints were fundamental. Brown served as Medical Superintendent in Bedlam from 1878–88. His was a reign of terror. Depending on the doctor, menstruation – and therefore sexual awakening – was seen as the root of all psychoses. Cures included attaching leeches to the vulva or, in more extreme cases, clitoridectomies and hysterectomies, popular with the dreaded Dr Brown.

Eliza did have poor mental health. She had already been admitted to Bedlam for mania a few times previously where she was described as being in a frenzied and incomprehensible state. Each time she did not stay long and was sent home 'cured'. However, when she was admitted at the age of 23 in 1857 after the stress of her maid's job, she was diagnosed as having melancholia and admitted to ward one, the ward for disruptive patients. Records show that she spent some time in the padded cell. Images of padded cells evoke feelings of horror but they were kinder than some of the terrible metal restraints used or heavy clothing in which your hands were sewn in to prevent you from harming yourself or anyone else. Eliza had arrived with injuries to her face and her stepmother said she had been trying to hurt herself.

To begin with reports suggested Eliza was getting better but she became more depressed and spent the rest of her life in the incurables ward. Who knows what treatments Eliza was given and if that had anything to do with her admittance to the incurables ward. The vast majority of us will suffer from poor mental health at some point in our lifetime and we can be thankful we won't be placed in the Bethlem of old, although there's still a long way to go.

Eliza Ruhamah Scidmore
(14 October 1856–3 November 1928)

Eliza was the first female board member of the National Geographic Society, a journalist, author, photographer, Japanese expert, plant-lover and social activist.

She was the daughter of parents who separated, her mother (also Eliza) running a boarding house in Washington DC during the Civil War. Her lawyer/diplomat brother George served across the Far East. With this family background, Eliza was never going to be your typical Victorian gentlewoman.

Born in Clinton, Iowa, she went to Oberlin College between 1873 and 1874 before moving to Washington DC to work as a society reporter at the age of 19, with her pieces appearing in papers including the *New York Times*. Even though that in itself was a huge and rare accomplishment for a young woman, it was never going to be enough for her. So she used her earnings to broaden her horizons.

Her first excursion in 1883 was to Alaska via a mail steamship with Captain James Carroll, and from here she wrote hugely popular articles for the American newspapers, later published in 1885 as the first travel guide to Alaska. Her adventures sound incredible – meeting Native Alaskan people the Tlingit and white settler Dick Willoughby. The Scidmore Glacier in Alaska is named in her honour for promoting Alaska to future travellers.

She must have been seen as scandalous; a highly intelligent, college-educated and unmarried woman travelling independently across the globe, clocking up miles to India, China, the Philippines, Java and Sri Lanka, not to mention actually writing for a living. Perish the thought!

The year 1885 proved to be game changer. Eliza went to Japan to visit her brother. And it was there that she completely and utterly fell in love. It was to be a life-long passion, particularly for its cherry trees ('sakura') and blossom, which she would describe as the 'most beautiful thing in the world'. She would return there frequently for work, pleasure and also as an informal ambassador for the US.

She introduced the word 'tsunami' to the rest of the world following her report of a devastating earthquake in 1896. She would write several travel books, cultural articles for magazines, including *Harper's Bazaar* and *Cosmopolitan*, and books, most notably a non-fiction account of the Russo-Japanese War.

The contacts she'd made in Washington DC would prove useful. She'd use them to bend the ear of First Lady Helen 'Nellie' Taft, who, together with Washington Park managers, supported her 24-year long ambition to bring 3,000 beautiful cherry trees, as a diplomatic gift from Mayor Yukio Ozaki of Tokyo, to be planted alongside the Potomac Basin in Washington in 1912. Eliza was a special guest of the First Lady, one of only three, at the private ceremony on 27 March in Potomac Park. That gift is now celebrated every year during the National Cherry Blossom Festival in Washington.

Eliza joined the National Geographic Society in 1890, two years after it was founded and pretty much had a finger in every pie – associate editor, foreign secretary, writer, photographer (she was a strong and early advocate of the first colour pictures in the magazine, many of which were hers) and lecturer.

Following complications from appendicitis, she died in Geneva, Switzerland in 1928 at the age of 72. Her ashes are kept in Yokohama, Japan with those of her mother and brother George. Hugely private, none of her personal letters remain – they were burnt by her family upon her death – and we are all the poorer for their loss.

Dame Emma Hamilton
(26 April 1765–15 January 1815)

The great and scandalous paramour of Admiral Lord Nelson, Emma Hamilton spent much of her life being passed around as a beautiful plaything between rich, aristocratic men.

She had no choice; she wouldn't have survived otherwise. That was the fate of women, including Amy or Emy Lyon, born 26 April 1765 in the poor pit village of Ness in Cheshire. Her father, blacksmith Henry Lyon, died soon after she was born, resulting in Amy and her mother Mary moving to a small cottage in Wales in extreme financial dire straits.

Beautiful, socially ambitious and determined to escape her poor background Amy headed to London in 1777 and found work as a maid, before working as a dancer at a Piccadilly brothel. In 1781, the now 16-year-old Amy was taken in by her lover Sir Harry Fetherstonehaugh, only to be abandoned by him when she became pregnant with their child. Utterly distraught, she pleaded for herself and her mother to be taken under the wing of another aristocrat, Charles Greville. He agreed, on the premise she change her name to Emma Hart and that once born the child be sent away. Her first-born daughter Emma Carew subsequently spent most of her life with her maternal great-grandmother Sarah Kidd in Wales.

Emma Hart would be mainly kept in social isolation by Greville, all the while unsuccessfully pleading for her daughter to live with them. He refused. During this time, she became a hugely popular artists' model, featuring in over sixty portraits by George Romney alone. Jealous of her celebrity, on 26 April 1786, Emma's 21st birthday, Greville handed her over to his uncle Sir William Hamilton, the British Ambassador to Naples, during a trip there that he pretended was a holiday. Upon their arrival, Greville abandoned her and informed her by letter that he wanted her to become Hamilton's mistress.

Fortunately for Emma, Hamilton treated her well. They grew to love each other and married in 1791. Emma, Lady Hamilton learned Italian, French and became a singer and accomplished musician. Their sumptuous social and diplomatic circles in Naples meant she became a great and close friend of Maria Carolina, Queen of Naples and Sicily, who was the sister of Marie Antoinette.

She and her husband would first meet and make friends with Horatio Nelson in September 1793 during the French Wars of Revolution. A few years later, in 1798, Emma played a vital role in helping secure a major victory for him; his naval forces were desperate for fresh supplies at St Peter, a major Sicilian port. Emma, using her close friendship with Maria Carolina, managed to get the supplies released in time for Nelson to win the Battle of the Nile.

Emma was also made a Dame of Malta by the Czar of Russia and given the Maltese Cross, the first English woman to be so honoured, for generously using her own funds to provide huge amounts of grain for the starving populace being blockaded by the French. By the following year, Emma and Nelson were besotted with each other, so much so that he joined her and her husband, in what must have been a jolly family trio, at the Hamiltons' rented home in Palermo, Sicily. On their eventual recall to England in 1800, the passionate affair continued. Emma became pregnant with twins.

Nelson's wife Fanny was banned from visiting him. Humiliated beyond endurance by Emma and Nelson's subsequent and very public affair, she gave Nelson an ultimatum. Furious at being challenged by his wife, our naval hero walked out on her. They would never see each other again. And that wasn't even what most scandalised society. Again proving that men could have their cake and eat it too, it was perfectly acceptable for high-flying society men like Nelson to take courtesans as lovers. What was a complete 'no-no' was actually leaving your wife for your mistress. Go-figure.

In 1801, Nelson and Emma's child Horatia was born. The other twin did not survive. They bought land in Surrey and planned to live there together, along with the ageing Sir William, who died in London in 1803.

On 21 October 1805, the British forces, led by Nelson on board his ship the *Victory*, would decimate the French and Spanish fleets at Trafalgar, near Cadiz. Wounded during the battle, Nelson died late in the afternoon of the 21st. Emma would only find out the news on 6 November. She was inconsolable and banned from the funeral.

It was downhill from there. Nelson's dying wishes for Emma and Horatia to be provided for were brutally ignored. She was shunned and, due to her luxurious lifestyle, left hugely in debt. She died in 1815, with Horatia by her side and was buried in an unmarked grave in the Church of St Pierre's in Calais.

Nelson, in comparison, was and is remembered as one of the great British heroes of all time, with a national monument, Nelson's Column, erected to commemorate his endeavours. Despite the fact that it was Nelson's 'column' that got Emma into trouble in the first place, she died impoverished, her spirit and heart broken, betrayed by the society which she had spent her life fighting to be accepted by. Ironically, their daughter Horatia Nelson would marry a clergyman and have a quiet, unremarkable life.

Empress Theodora
(*c.* 500–48)

Empress Theodora of Constantinople really was a regular Byzantine fairytale Cinderella. Daddy was a poor bear keeper at Constantinople's Hippodrome which, startlingly, was not the lusted-after job it might sound like. After he died the family's situation became desperate. So Theodora and her sisters took to the stage.

Theodora worked as an actress, dancer, mime artist and comedian; and back in those heady days of 'Constantinople's Got Talent', actresses were expected to give audience members a bit of 'knickers down' after the curtain fell. (Today's luvvies don't appreciate the association 'actress' then had with 'hooker', so now insist on being called an 'actor'.) It's likely Theodora was no exception. However, it's doubtful she was the depraved sexual monster painted by her biographer Procopius in his book *The Secret History*, written after her death. Indeed much of his lurid details about her early years probably owe more to his own lewd imagination than to actual fact. *50 Shades of Grey* has nothing on the images he paints of Theodora, one example being of one night spent with thirty men and some geese. (Sounds exhausting.)

But like a good Cinderella, Theodora shut her legs for business and discovered God during a brief sojourn in Libya. From that point the fair Prince Justininan was fated to fall in love with her and persuade the powers to be to change the law prohibiting actresses to marry. (Something modern-day actresses have taken to with gusto.)

Through a series of courtly machinations, twists, turns and political conspiracies, she and her husband became emperor and empress, a true power couple in the mould of Hilary and Bill Clinton. Her radical reforms included laws to protect women at risk such as her former friends engaged in prostitution and making rape punishable by death, making Theodora one of our firm early feminist favourites.

Empress Wu Zetian
(624–705)

The only woman in Chinese history to rule as an empress, doing so during the Tang Dynasty (AD 618–906), which was a relatively 'good' time for women in China – there was no binding of feet and a lot more freedom. The period of the Tang Dynasty's power is widely regarded as the golden age of Chinese history, which says much for the empress's achievements, despite attempts by historians to paint her as a villain, tyrant and all-round dragon lady.

Whu Zhao, daughter to a wealthy dad and well-connected mum, became concubine number 5 to the 40-year-old Emperor Taizong when she was just 13. Being number 5 out of 9 didn't sit well with this particular girl's ambitions, but it was nothing a little murder and Machiavellian mischief wouldn't solve.

She raced up that ladder very quickly, and following Taizong's death was recalled from a convent to marry his son and successor Emperor Li Zhi Gaozong. Interestingly they'd already been having an affair. Our girl clearly believed in planning ahead. They had a baby girl who was allegedly strangled, allowing Wu to neatly and rather conveniently remove the former Empress Wang from the political equation and have her killed.

She became huanghou, or empress. Gaozong's frequent ill health and subsequent stroke in 690, five years into their marriage, and her poisoning her eldest son Li Hong, led her to assume the full powers of the emperor in 690 at the age of 65.

What followed was a three-year reign of 'Soprano'-inspired terror, complete with a secret police force, where she ruthlessly murdered or framed innocent victims, forced suicides and generally raised hell with anyone who opposed her. She did whatever was politically expedient. Perhaps if she'd been a man her actions would have been viewed differently. She was also an alleged nymphomaniac who liked observing herself with lovers in mirrors, but that's conjecture and possibly propaganda.

Why did a woman, much less a former concubine, get away with this? Because the people loved her: she brought peace and prosperity during her dynasty by rooting out corruption and helping the common people. She stepped down from the throne in 705 in favour of her third son and died later that year. Her tomb remains unopened, her tombstone mysteriously left blank.

Flora Sandes
(22 January 1876–24 November 1956)

Flora Sandes defies stereotypes. The only woman permitted to enlist in the First World War as a soldier, she is frequently described in masculine terms. However, whilst Flora enjoyed so-called male pursuits, she also loved shopping and a good party.

She didn't give a fig for what society thought, perhaps thanks to a happy, liberal childhood that let Flora enjoy her favourite activities – hunting, shooting and reading adventure stories. As an adult she loved 'galumphing' (getting drunk), smoking (a lot) and travelling. Her nephew Dick believed she could drink more than the average man. Heaven knows what Dick would have made of the antics of the average twenty-first-century Glasgow girl.

She famously said that as a child she wished she had been born a boy, but the truth is, like so many, she was a frustrated woman born in the wrong time, an early feminist desperate for the same freedoms her brothers enjoyed. She participated eagerly in various suffrage movements as well as the FANY (First Aid Nursing Yeomanry), and these were the days before a fanny was a 'fanny', enabling her to gain wartime first-aid skills. She then joined the St John Ambulance Brigade.

One of the first to sign up as a volunteer (now aged 40), she was frustrated to be turned away from many voluntary corps, due her suffrage past giving her a label of troublesome coupled with a lack of formal training, denied her because she was too posh for that sort of malarkey.

She was finally accepted into Mabel Grouitch's Corps which was bound for Serbia due to a shortage of trained surgeons and nurses. The three-week journey there was uncomfortable, exhausting and riddled with problems but she still managed to kick her heels up with Emily Simmonds, her new BFF. Her fellow nurses may have been horrified by their risqué behaviour but by the time they reached Serbia, Flora was all business. Despite being told she wouldn't survive a month, she volunteered to help at Valjevo, a town stricken by typhus, which she nearly died from herself. As the fighting grew worse, she then enlisted in the Serbian army.

There are numerous examples of her bravery, stoicism and cheerfulness in the face of desperate hardship and danger. However the daring escapade that won Flora the highest honour in the Serbian army, the Kara George Medal, a promotion to sergeant major and a hero's write-up in most national papers in Britain was the tale of her being wounded by a grenade whilst leading her men in Macedonia. She had to be dragged through no man's land to safety, her right arm shattered by the grenade.

Like so many of the fiercely brave women who volunteered on the front line, Flora returned home to find the freedoms enjoyed during the war swiftly curtailed by a country eager to put women back in their place. Flora retired to her home town of Suffolk where she carried on being the racy, hell-bent rebel she had always been in her electric wheelchair.

Golda Meir
(3 May 1898–8 December 1978)

Golda was the fourth Prime Minister of Israel and its first female premier.

Born in Russia as Goldie Mabovitch, her family fled Kiev (now capital of Ukraine) to escape pogroms and violent massacres of Jews – she witnessed her father boarding up the front door in anticipation of them. The family moved to Wisconsin in the US in 1906 and, against the wishes of her parents, Golda trained as a teacher in Milwaukee in 1917. A passionate and active leader of the Milwaukee Zionist Party, she married Morris Myers in 1917. They emigrated to Palestine in 1921 and joined the Merhavya kibbutz; she and Morris would separate but never divorce.

Golda was of only three women to sign Israel's historic Declaration of Independence; in an ironic twist, considering her place of birth and reasons for fleeing it, she was made ambassador to the Soviet Union. Strong, tough, dependable and passionately protective of the Jewish people, in May 1948 she went to Jordan disguised as a Muslim man to try and persuade King Abdullah not to attack Israel. Elected to the Israeli Knesset, or government, in 1949 (she would remain a member until 1974), she was made Labour Minister by Prime Minister David Ben-Gurion. The remit of this post, which she held from 1949–56, was enormous: in the aftermath of the Second World War and the Holocaust she was charged with finding housing and jobs for the hundreds of thousands of immigrants pouring into the new State of Israel. She also convinced the American Jewish community to put $50 million towards securing the fledgling state's security against their Arab neighbours.

Ben-Gurion referred to Golda as 'the best man' in his cabinet and appointed her Foreign Minister in 1956, effectively his Number Two. He also advised her to embrace her new Israeli citizenship and change her surname from Myerson to Meir. Ten years later, she stepped down at a time when she was also secretly being treated for lymphoma, a fact that would only become public after her death.

Following the death of Prime Minister Levi Eshkol in 1969, she came out of retirement to take on the role of Prime Minister at the age of 71. That very rare thing, a woman in power, in the Middle East no less, she took to the international political stage to push hard for peace via diplomacy.

Her efforts would be dramatically stalled by the onset of the Fourth Arab-Israeli War in 6 October 1973, when Egypt (led by President Anwar el-Sadat) and Syria launched a joint surprise attack on the fledgling state on the most holy date in the Jewish calendar: Yom Kippur, or the Day of Atonement, when most members of the IDF (Israeli Defence Force) would be off duty. Iraq and Jordan would also join in the fight against Israel, which swiftly fought back. The United Nations organised a ceasefire on 25 October.

Israel hadn't been prepared and suffered heavy losses: Golda took the blame and eventually stepped down in April 1974 to be succeeded by Yitzhak Rabin. She died in Jerusalem on 8 December 1978.

Gorgo
(AD 508/518?–?)

The second of the Spartan women featured in this book is Gorgo. We don't know much about her, but like Aspasia the fact we know about her at all speaks volumes.

Daughter of Cleomenes I, King of Sparta, she would have been raised at her father's court and been accomplished in singing and dancing. Spartan women had a much better deal than their Athenian counterparts. They had greater freedoms, could have an education and own land. They didn't usually marry until they were between 18 and 20 years old and they could inherit.

Gorgo married her father's half-brother (making him her half-uncle) King Leonidas I. Together they had a son, Pleistarchus, co-King of Sparta from 480 BC to his death in 458 BC. According to Plutarch, 'When asked by a woman from Attica, "Why are you Spartan women the only ones who can rule men?", she said: "Because we are also the only ones who give birth to men."'

According to Herodotus, Gorgo was born either in 518 or 508 BC; we don't know when she died but it's likely she had married Leonidas by 490 BC and was still alive when he died at Thermopylae in 480 BC alongside his famous and, if Hollywood is anything to go by, incredibly fit 300 warriors.

Wise and politically astute, both her father and her husband took her advice on board. That Herodotus mentions her being present at her father's diplomatic meetings is even more extraordinary considering she was female. She outsmarted the Persians by working out a secret code sent on a writing tablet (not the Apple or MacBook variety) that had been cleverly covered with melted wax.

She must have indeed been a great woman of note, although after her husband's death, she disappears from history. Just think how many women like Gorgo lived – but died in obscurity and we know nothing of them.

Grace Humiston
(17 September 1867–16 July 1948)

When you type Grace Humiston into a search engine, a gratifying number of pages appear about her life as a private investigator. It's a shame though that the name dominating these searches is 'Mrs Sherlock Holmes', a nickname bestowed by the press. Grace's accomplishments should be enough without being subsumed as an appendage to a fictional male hero.

She graduated from the New York School of Law in 1904, no mean feat for a woman during the Edwardian era. That was the least of her achievements. She was a passionate activist for the poor and marginalised, especially immigrants, and set up a legal agency called the People's Law Firm, providing pro bono services.

Like a legal superhero she rooted out corruption, espionage, murder and slavery. After being asked to investigate several disappearances of immigrants, she followed a lead that took her to a ring of nasty forced labour camps in the South. The immigrants had been enticed to come and then forced to stay. Incognito, she risked visiting these camps, sometimes in disguise, to uncover the truth. Her work led to her being made the first female Special Assistant US Attorney giving her the power to prosecute the people involved.

Grace also helped many wrongfully convicted people, saving them from Death Row. In 1916 she helped Charles Stielow, who had been sentenced to death after some damning evidence. With just 40 minutes until he was scheduled to die, Grace and her team were able to get a stay of execution giving them the time to find the real killer. We've seen this type of story played out ad nauseam on formulaic TV shows, but this was the real deal and achieved by an Edwardian woman no less.

Her most famous case involved the disappearance of Ruth Cruger. This 18-year-old girl went missing on 13 February 1917, after taking her ice skates to be mended at a motorcycle repair shop run by Alfredo Cocchi. Despite a public campaign, the police failed to find her and claimed that she was immoral and had run off. Enraged, Ruth's father hired Grace to pick up their slack. She was convinced that the young woman had been murdered and her body hidden in the city. They discovered that Cocchi had a rap sheet for assault on women and had conveniently run away to Italy. His wife refused to let Grace dig up their cellar so Grace got permission to dig up the sidewalk just outside the shop on health and safety grounds. Lo and behold some of Ruth's personal items were found. After that there was no impediment to digging up the cellar revealing Ruth's body.

Grace then went after the NYPD for negligence and corruption – it was quite the embarrassment for the men in blue. Crucially the case undermined prevalent attitudes that all missing girls were of bad character and had run away to a life of shame. She went on to fight campaigns for missing girls and the slipshod way their cases were treated.

Despite her fame and the press coverage garnered during this time, Grace faded into obscurity. An investigation in 1917 accusing some soldiers of abusing women backfired and became a scandal. During the First World War there was strong nationalist fervour and it was not the ideal time to level accusations at the army. The public took against her and the army savagely kicked her off the pedestal that they had put her on so recently. She carried on supporting causes but her name was no longer respected and her own story became as neglected and forgotten as the missing girls she had tried to save.

Gráinne Ní Mháille, aka Grace O'Malley, Queen of Umail and the Pirate Queen of Ireland (*c.* 1530–1603)

The sixteenth century saw the rise of two queens, both fearless, ruthless and awe-inspiring – you would not want to mess with either of these formidable women.

They were Queen Elizabeth I and, the relatively unknown, Grace O'Malley, chieftain of the west coast of Ireland. Tensions between the Gaelic Irish and the English would bring those two women face to face.

Grace's tenacious spirit was evident from a young age. When her father, chieftain of the kingdom of Umhall, banned her from sailing with him on a trading expedition, she refused to take no for an answer. Her mother wrung her hands and warned her wayward daughter that her long hair would get trapped in the ropes. Grace responded by chopping off her hair and boarding the merchant ship – problem solved. This wasn't just an isolated teenage transgression; this was a sign of the fierce, independent women she would become – from teen to OAP rebellion.

Grace O'Malley was the sort of woman you admire but may not cosy up with. She was of the Enid Blyton and games teacher ilk – the pull yourself up by the boot straps and get on with it type. Swashbuckling tales and legends abound about Grace, such as one about a sea battle where she admonishes her son to stop cowardly hiding behind her petticoats whilst she brandishes swords and fury. She wasn't a fan of maternity leave either, as just one day after giving birth on her ship she took up arms to defend it before berating useless men who couldn't let her have one day off without needing her.

She was a fiercely protective mother hen protecting not just her own children but also her vast brood of clansmen. Gaelic Ireland was disintegrating and being swallowed up by Tudor England. The clans that had enjoyed autonomy were fighting the English, fighting each other or giving in and swearing fealty to Henry VIII as their king in return for a title and land.

Grace's family being of the same tough bootstrap genes was disgusted by those who appeased the English and when the patriarchal Gaelic system tried to stop Grace inheriting her father's ships, she soon put paid to their misogynistic nonsense by showing her fearsome mettle.

She was in charge of hundreds of men and a fleet of ships as well as commanding a land army to protect her territory from the English. In a highly successful highway robbery of the seas, her men would demand 'tax' from ships that sailed in their waters. Refusal turned the seawater red, earning her such a fearsome reputation that the English decided it was time to deal with the Gaelic Pirate Queen.

After laying siege to her castle in Rockfleet in 1574, the English soon turned tail and ran after she chased them off. They now saw her as a serious threat to the anglicising of Ireland and their hope for a shiny new green land. Sir Richard Bingham, the English governor of Connaugh, was more tenacious and succeeded in taking her castle, cattle and basically making a rather dangerous nuisance of himself. So what do you do when middle management doesn't listen? You bypass them for the big boss. Grace took herself off to London to plead her case to Queen Elizabeth I, a bold move as she was a wanted pirate facing a gruesome execution from a queen who was not known for her forgiving nature.

Grace was a canny lass and could play court politics with the best of them, and somehow persuaded the good queen to order her castle and lands be handed back to her and to legitimise her seafaring 'business'. There may have been some agreement that Grace would help keep the even more 'annoying' Spanish at bay, but, as ever, there are few records left to say exactly what went on.

Sources claim that Grace realised quite correctly that her new pal Elizabeth was likely to renege on the deal. However, Grace managed to live to a ripe old age and died in around 1603 in Rockfleet Castle. Her legend continues to this day.

Gracia Mendes Nasi
(1510–69)

Dona Gracia, known as 'La Señora', was an immensely wealthy Jewish woman who lived during the European Renaissance. Her inspirational story is one of political intrigue, religious freedom and fortune. She is remembered as a 'Saviour of the Jews' and was arguably one of the richest women in the world at the time.

Her Jewish noble family were originally from Aragon, Spain, with the surname 'Nasi', Hebrew for 'prince'. Upon being thrown out of the country in 1492 by Catholic Queen Isabella and King Ferdinand, they were forcibly baptised in Portugal in around 1497. As a 'Conversos', or 'Marranos', 'de Luna' would be their Christian name and Beatrice was born in 1510.

In 1528, in a big, public and very Catholic wedding, Beatrice married fellow Converso Francisco Mendes Benveniste, a hugely prosperous international gem and spice merchant in Lisbon. They would have a secret Jewish ceremony later. He died in 1535, leaving her with their 5-year-old daughter Reyna and half of his huge fortune.

Shortly afterwards, on May 23 1536, the Pope established a Portuguese Inquisition, based on the terrifying Spanish version. This was an absolute disaster for families like the Mendes and Nasis who whilst outwardly conforming to Catholic traditions, secretly practised Judaism. If found out, their fortunes would be confiscated and their lives put at grave risk.

Beatrice promptly upped sticks, took the young Reyna and her own sister Brianda and fled to Antwerp (then part of Flanders) to join Diogo Mendes, Francisco's brother and business partner, who had expanded the family fortune into the banking industry. Beatrice would use the money business to help other Jewish Conversos escape from Portugal, ingeniously filtering their money through a secret financial network, enabling them to start new lives elsewhere. It's likely that her status as a widow gave her independence, a bonus she wasn't prepared to give up. She never remarried.

Her sister Brianda, however, went on to marry Diogo and when he died, he also left half his fortune to Beatrice, making her a hugely wealthy, independent Jewish woman. Whilst his actions say much for his respect for Beatrice's business acumen, it really put the cat amongst the pigeons between the sisters.

Back to the Inquisition, made up of a tricky bunch of religious fanatics, which had extended its long tentacles into Spanish-owned Antwerp, home of the Mendes family as well as many other Jewish Conversos. Francisco might very well have been dead and buried, but it wasn't going to stop them pursuing him for pretending to be a Catholic whilst hiding his true Jewish roots. Of course they also wanted to get their grubby little hands on his fortune but they hadn't reckoned with the brains of Beatrice. She 'loaned' a huge amount of cash to Emperor Charles V to keep him happy. Then of course, there were the fortune hunters out for daughter Reyna's hand in marriage.

It was time to flee, once again, this time to Venice and then in time to the Duchy of Ferrara, where they could live freely as Jews with other Conversos from Portugal.

As such, Beatrice felt secure enough to change her name to Dona Gracia Nasi, 'Gracia' the Hebrew name for Hannah (meaning 'grace') and Nasi (meaning 'prince'). From her new home she would use her considerable wealth and contacts to continue to rescue fellow Jews from the claws of the Inquisition and get them out of Portugal. She was also responsible for the eight-month boycott of the Italian port of Ancona, after Jewish merchants were captured, tortured and burned there, and some sold into slavery. She also paid for Hebrew books, including the Bible, to be printed in Spanish, much easier for the Conversos to use.

She would return to Venice before moving once more to Constantinople where she became a leading patron of the Jewish community, establishing a yeshiva (a Jewish seminary for men), synagogue, schools and hospitals. She also continued the family business, trading goods with her own fleet of ships. La Señora died in 1569.

Harriet Beecher Stowe
(14 June 1811–1 July 1896)

It's impossible to view Harriet's life without considering the collective influence of her liberal family, who symbolised a shining light in an era of Civil War, slavery and social unrest.

Born in Litchfield, Connecticut on 14 June 1811, she was one of nine children born to preacher Lyman Beecher and Roxanna Foote Beecher. (Another three children were added to the mix when, following the death of Roxanna, Lyman married again.)

The household was big on education; all of Harriet's seven brothers became ministers; her sister Isabella was an important part of the burgeoning women's rights movement, organising the annual convention of the National Woman's Suffrage Association in 1871. Together with her husband, Isabella was also integral in pushing through a Connecticut piece of legislation in 1877 which gave married women the same rights as their husbands.

Harriet's other sister Catharine was a teacher at Hartford Female Seminary, a progressive school in Connecticut (Harriet attended from the age of 13), which believed in academic education for girls as opposed to equipping them with more traditional feminine accomplishments. Catharine also established schools in Ohio, Illinois and Wisconsin.

Harriet herself published over thirty books, fiction, non-fiction, essays and poems. Her most famous publication is *Uncle Tom's Cabin*, or *Life Among the Lowly*, which played an important part in fuelling the anti-slavery fervour which led to the eventual abolishment of slavery in the US. Based on the accounts of escaped slaves including Josiah Henson, its first instalment was published in the anti-slavery newspaper, the *National Era*, on 5 June 1851. It was then published as a two-volume book the following year and was a best seller. In its first year, 300,000 copies sold in the US and 1.5 million in Britain.

Harriet established schools for slaves and supported the Underground Railroad – the secret network used to help African American slaves to escape into free states or Canada. At the outbreak of the Civil War she travelled to Washington DC and met Abraham Lincoln at the White House, encouraging him to move swiftly to end slavery. Family legend has it that Mr Lincoln, referring to the war between the North and the South (12 April 1861–9 May 1865), said to her: 'So you are the little woman who wrote the book that started this great war.'

She married Calvin Stowe, a professor of theology who taught at Andover Theological Seminary between 1853 and 1864. An outbreak of cholera killed their youngest son Samuel Charles in 1849; their third son Henry drowned, fourth son Frederick disappeared on his way to California and daughter Georgiana died from a morphine-addiction related illness. Harriet died in Hartford, Connecticut on 1 July 1896 at the age of 85.

Hatshepsut
(1508–1458 BC)

The second female pharaoh (Sobekneferu was the first; fourteen centuries after Hatshepsut, Cleopatra would be the third and last), Hatshepsut (her name means 'foremost of noblewomen') was the longest reigning (twenty-two years) Queen of Egypt.

She became queen when she married her half-brother Thutmose II, the son of her father and one of his wives. Whilst they had a daughter together, Neferure, on her brother's death, the throne went to Thutmose III, Thutmose II's son with another of his wives, and Hatshepsut became regent. She appointed herself co-ruler three years later effectively becoming a pharaoh in her own right as a woman.

A brilliant political operator, she would manipulate her image to suit her ends, having herself depicted as a strong-bearded and muscled male in various images and statues and reverting to a female form when that was more beneficial to her requirements. However, following her death, Thutmose III vandalised, defaced (by chiselling off her name) and destroyed many of her statues, probably in an effort to de-legitimise her role as a female ruler or allow himself to take the credit for her successes.

During her reign, the temple at Deir el-Bahri was constructed and she organised a hugely successful trading trip to Punt, probably located between today's Ethiopia and Sudan. She is buried in the Valley of Kings. Her mummy, discovered in 2007 and now kept in Cairo's Egyptian Museum, revealed that she was overweight, probably had diabetes, had bald patches and wore black and red nail varnish.

Hedy Lamarr
(9 November 1914–19 January 2000)

Hedy Lamarr was the archetypal sex siren of the golden screen. She was famously described as the most beautiful woman in the world and this often seemed to be the sole reason for her featuring in Hollywood films. Her acting ability was not as promising as her face but in tinsel town as long as the tinsel sparkles, who cares that it's only ornamental. And so Hedy has often been dismissed as just another gorgeous gal. But there was so much more to her than that.

Hedy's real life was far more interesting and action-packed than many of her films. She had a controversial career in Germany where she appeared nude in the film *Ecstasy* in 1933. That was bad enough but she was also filmed enjoying an orgasm – surely orgasms were not invented until the 1970s? Nevertheless, behind her artificially enhanced chest lay the sole of a science nerd. Being a good Jewish girl (OK, she was brought up Catholic) Hedy married a Jewish boy but he was far from good and not very happy about being Jewish. They lived in Vienna and his munitions business led him to cosy up with Hitler, Mussolini and their ilk, including doing the Fuhrer quick step at extravagant parties in their home.

Hedy complained that he controlled every aspect of her life and kept her in a gilded cage. However his insistence on bringing her to business meetings where munitions and warfare were the headline on the agenda armed her with some serious tech know-how. She ran away from him and ended up in Paris where she met Louis B. Goldmayer and was swept off to La La Land.

She was cast in famous yet less intellectually challenging roles that required little more than sexy smouldering. Not so surprisingly she found this all a bit tedious and turned her brain to inventions behind the scenes. It was during this time that she met the famous pianist and composer George Antheil at a dinner party. She went on to collaborate with him in making a secret, jam-proof radio-guidance system for the Allies to use in the Second World War. For fellow science buffs the system used spread spectrum and frequency hopping in a method similar to how piano rolls operate. However, and you will be shocked by this, the US Navy didn't want to know and dismissed her work until the 1960s when the Cuban Missile Crisis erupted. Hedy was persuaded she would be more useful to the Allies by using her star status to sell war bonds, raising $7 million.

This technology has become the basis of the Wi-Fi and Bluetooth technology we know today. It took years for her contribution to be recognised, a fact that may have contributed to her later feelings of bitterness. She was arrested for shoplifting several times – one can only imagine the psychological background to those actions. However in 1997 she and George Antheil were finally presented with prestigious awards to mark their vital scientific contributions. But it was not until 2014 that they were added to the national Inventors Hall of Fame.

Hester Stanhope
(12 March 1776–23 June 1839)

British eccentrics don't come better than Hester. An adventuress with a deluded sense of grandeur which would prove her downfall, Hester was one hell of a woman. Byron once famously referred to her as 'that dangerous thing, a female wit'.

Being an aristocrat was not her bag. Instead, in 1810 at the age of 33, this granddaughter of William Pitt the Elder and niece of Prime Minister William Pitt the Younger (she acted as his official hostess for a while at Downing Street) decided to embark on a mind-boggling, frankly awesome expedition across the Middle East. Enriched, thanks to her uncle, with a generous pension of £1,200 from the British government, she would never return home again.

She visited Turkey, Greece and the Middle East. She learned Arabic and Turkish, adopted Turkish man's clothes and rode on horseback into the city of Damascus bare-headed. Unthinkable. Yet her chutzpah, arrogance and self-belief were so intense that she was treated as a queen.

Her life was literally a whirlwind of shipwrecks, younger lovers (Michael Bruce, twelve years her junior), public executions (not her own, obviously, but watching others), investments in archaeological digs (Ashkelon, Israel) and meeting with sultans, sheiks, emirs and downright bloodthirsty tyrants and criminals.

In her later years she developed a messianic, megalamaniac, Trump-esque zeal and conviction that she had been chosen for greatness to be 'Queen of the Jews'. And not just because a former inmate of Bedlam had told her so. Let's take one of her quotes: 'I have nothing to fear . . . I am the sun, the stars, the pearl, the lion, the light from heaven'.

Decades before ISIS would desecrate it, she became the first white woman to enter the incredible Syrian city of Palmrya, once ruled by the mighty Zenobia. And she got there by traversing 60 miles of desert with a tribe of Bedouin. Always spending above her means, she borrowed huge amounts of money to open her home in Joun to the many refugees fleeing a brutal civil war.

She ended her days alone in a mountainous Lebanese fortress, which she'd adapted into her own personal kingdom (she'd also boarded it shut against the many moneylenders looking for payback), completely broke, very likely addicted to a local drug, completely out of her mind and an embarrassment to the British government, who'd had to cancel her pension in order to calm an irate Turkish creditor. Still, what a way to go.

Huda Shaarawi
(23 June 1879–12 December 1947)

As Egypt's first recognised feminist Huda was responsible for literally lifting the veil from the eyes of her fellow country women.

Nur al-Huda Sultan was born into a wealthy and politically important family in Cairo, raised in a secluded harem guarded by eunuchs. The harem, whilst not the opulent den of sexual iniquity often portrayed in Western literature, was more a patriarchal demonstration of wealth. Only the very rich could afford to run a completely separate household just for the women of the family. Their education was restricted (although Huda would learn Arabic, French and Turkish at home and  how to play the piano) and there was a strong line of separation between what the men and women of the household were allowed to do.

She was married off in 1892 when she was just 13 to an older cousin, Ali Shaarawi. That Huda didn't want to get married was irrelevant. She had no choice. It was just the way things were done and refusal would mean shame for her family. She would also only be her husband's second wife; he was already married with children. A woman's sphere was the home or the harem and their lives were insufferably restricted. The men were in charge. Even when they did leave the harem, they had to wear a veil.

After fifteen months of marriage, having been banned from piano playing by her new husband or visiting her family, Huda went home; she and Ali would live separate lives for seven years of their marriage. During those years of independence, probably available to her because of her family's wealth and social standing, Huda educated herself thoroughly and attended cultural salons headed by prominent feminists.

Her marriage to Ali would resume as a partnership when Huda was 21. He took her to Paris where her eyes were opened to the freedoms of European women. They would have two children, daughter Bathna (born in 1903) and son Muhammad (born in 1905).

Starting as she most definitely meant to go on, and with the support of Egyptian Princess Ain al-Hayat, Huda set up a women's charity in 1908, the first Egyptian Philanthropic Society. She followed this by opening a school two years later. Standing alongside her fellow Egyptian women, Huda would go on to campaign vociferously against British occupation, on one occasion facing armed British soldiers in a 3-hour stand-off, with a gun literally held to her head as she dared them to shoot her and make her the Egyptian version of English heroine and spy Edith Cavell.

Ali served as treasurer of the Egyptian nationalist Wafd Party whilst Huda was elected president of the Wafdist Women's Central Committee in 1920. Their joint political interests created a strong and mutually respectful partnership. He would die in February 1922.

Huda went on to travel across the globe to campaign at international women's congresses. It was on her return from one of these meetings, the International Women's Suffrage Alliance, in 1923 that she dramatically removed her veil in public at Cairo train station. The move was equally shocking and inspirational in its two-fingered salute to tradition. Many other women at the station applauded and followed suit; Huda would never wear the veil again.

That same year she founded and became president of the Egyptian Feminist Union; it published its own feminist magazine, *l'Egyptienne* (*el-Masreyya*) and fought passionately to change how women in Egypt lived. Keenly aware of Huda's forced marriage at 13, the Union campaigned against polygamy, for the minimum age of marriage for women to increase to 16 and for improved education and welfare reform. Huda died in 1947, having been awarded Egypt's highest honour, the Nishan al-Kamal, in 1945.

Hypatia
(*c.* 350/370–415/416)

The first female mathematician and astronomer in recorded history travelled to school by horse and chariot. Highly respected, an inventor and philosopher, her name was Hypatia.

She was Egyptian, lived in Alexandria in the fifth century AD and was probably one of the last scientists to have access to the books of the famous Library of Alexandria. She never married, dedicating her life to study and her students. A tenth-century encyclopaedia refers to her as: 'exceedingly beautiful and fair of form . . . in speech articulate and logical, in her actions prudent and public-spirited, and the rest of the city gave her suitable welcome and accorded her special respect'.

None of her work survived. No notebooks. Nothing. There's no information on her mother – because the women of the time weren't seen as important enough to preserve in history. We only know about her father Theon, who was her teacher. Legend has it that he was determined to mould her into a perfect human being and encouraged her to stay fit through sport and physical activity. He was also the last recorded member of the Museum of Alexandria – which was very much like a modern-day university, with schools and public auditoriums. Students came from as far afield as Ethiopia and India to hear lectures on science and philosophy.

Hypatia's books on mathematics include the thirteen-volume *Commentary on the Arithmetica of Diophantus* (generally regarded as the father of algebra) as well as a book on astronomy, *The Astronomical Canon.* Much of what we know of Hypatia is from letters written by her most famous student Synesius of Cyrene, who later became the Bishop of Ptolemy. One suggests that her lectures included instructions on how to design an astrolabe, a type of portable astronomical calculator that would be used until the nineteenth century.

Too modern for the ancient world, Hypatia was murdered on the steps of a church in March 415. She was 45. She was stripped naked, brutally butchered with roofing tiles and then burnt by a mob of religious fanatics led by Peter the Lector, convinced that her way of thinking, Neo-Platonism, was heresy and a danger to Christianity.

She was probably also killed for being a friend of the governor of Alexandria, a man called Orestes, who was at odds with Cyril, the city's Archbishop. Rumours were spread that Hypatia was to blame for the two men fighting with each other. And for being a woman – a female teacher who encouraged her students to think about science and the wider world, the stars, the planets, the sun and the moon. (A huge asteroid in space is named after her.)

Some historians say that she was the first famous 'witch' to be punished for her beliefs. Many women of science were seen as witches. Men didn't like it. They didn't like women thinking for themselves.

Ida (24 August 1904–22 December 1986) and Louise Cook (19 June 1901–27 March 1991)

Ida and Louise Cook were two unassuming English women, ordinary clerical workers in London's grey rat race. But after their 9-to-5 day their lives turned Technicolour – alive with intrigue, danger and, above all, opera. Whilst this is a story about two intrepid heroines who saved the lives of twenty-nine families from Nazi Germany, their tales of derring-do cannot be separated from their obsession with the flamboyant world of opera.

It was opera that alerted them to the abhorrent crisis facing Germany's Jews in the 1930s and opera that gave them the means to fool German officials and save lives. They are now honoured as Righteous Gentiles by Yad Vashem.

And, oh my, did those gals love their opera – they were the 1920s' giddiest groupies! They scrimped and saved to raise money to buy a gramophone. Then they scrimped some more to pay their passage to New York and hear Amelita Galli-Curci sing live – oh, the thrill of it all. Dressed in homemade clothes and Woolworths accessories, they charmed their way into their idols' lives. Using her beloved Brownie camera, Ida captured them all for their own private pin-up collection.

During one trip to Salzburg in 1934, when the girls went to see their famous opera friends Clemen Kraus and his wife Viorica Ursuleac, they unwittingly brought their first refugee home. Kraus and Ursuelac brought Mitia Mayer-Lismann to the station to meet Ida and Louise. And the girls suspected nothing when they were asked to accompany her back to Britain. It was only later that they realised the danger Mitia had escaped.

The girls were not immune to the horrific atmosphere permeating Austria and Germany but now they were up close and personal. The ingenuity and self-sacrifice that had taken them to New York helped them navigate Hitler's horrifying world. Luckily Ida would soon assume the persona of Mary Burchell, one of the most prolific writers for Mills & Boon, and use the money she earned from that to finance their rescue missions. She still ended up in terrible debt, pouring all her money into the refugee situation.

Pretending to be dotty, opera-mad spinsters, they slipped past guards regularly. To smuggle the refugees' only means of raising money they would sew English labels on the escapees' fur coats and pretend their diamond jewels were paste gems from Woolworths whilst wearing them over the border. Kraus and Ursuelac, now working for the Berlin opera, played a crucial role. They let Ida and Louise know which operas were playing and when so their stories sounded completely plausible.

It was opera that got them through the dark days. When they were at their lowest, unable to save so many desperate people, when they had witnessed the endless suicides and brutality and knew so many families they couldn't save were going to the gas chambers, the girls would think of Rosa Ponselle, their favourite opera singer, and tell themselves those heady New York days would come again.

Ida's outgoing personality and work as a writer mean the stories are told in her voice but she credits Louise as much as herself. Louise's words are harder to find. After Ida's death in 1986, Louise burned all the letters and photos belonging to their intrepid past. Was she terribly grief-stricken and couldn't bear reminders or did she have a more damaged relationship with the past? It is a terrible shame that we will never know.

Isabel Godin des Odonais
(1728–92)

A desperate exploration of the Amazon, estranged lovers reunited, peril, betrayal, death and, above all else, survival – you could make it up but why bother when history has such epic tales hidden in its pages?

Nowadays it's practically a cliché to don a backpack and go exploring but we go armed with vaccinations, mosquito repellent, maps and sun screen. It was an entirely different proposition in the seventeenth century not least for genteel ladies brought up to delicately fan themselves while outside. The most seasoned of explorers thought twice before taking on the well-reputed dangers of the Amazon.

Isabel Godin would prove the dainty exception to this stereotyped rule. She was born in the Spanish colonial city Riobamba in 1728, now part of Ecuador. When the French arrived as part of an expedition to measure the equator under the famous La Contamine, she met Jean Godin des Odonais who had been employed as a chain-bearer (official measurer). They fell in love and married when she was only 13, the same age as Juliet when she fell for Romeo. Isabel and Jean would have a happier ending but there would be a wealth of tragedy along the way.

After Jean heard of his father's death, he decided it was time to return to France. Jean went on ahead as Isabel was pregnant, leaving her to book a safe passage home. When he tried to return to Riobamba, he was prevented by a bureaucratic nightmare. The Portuguese and Spanish had locked horns over territory and neither would allow a Frenchman through to collect his family. Now the romantic couple were separated by an entire continent, instead of contending with the feuding Capulets and Montagues, their love was sabotaged by feuding nations. He stayed and pestered endlessly, even a sending a desperate missive to the French government to suggest it was a good time for France to invade and take their land.

It would be twenty years before they held each other again. Eventually the King of Portugal decided a French ally would be helpful and agreed to send a ship to Isabel but Jean was paranoid the king had discovered his idea to go to war and that it was a trap. He sent his friend Tristan instead with money and letters, but the treacherous Tristan ran off with the money.

Isabel had heard rumours of this ship and sent her loyal slave Joaquin to investigate, promising him his freedom when she reunited with Jean. It took him two years to return and she decided she would meet that ship come hell or Amazonian water. Woefully naive, she set off in 1769 with a party of forty-two including servants to carry elaborate crockery, clothes and jewels – very handy in the rainforest, nothing like an emerald pendant for frightening away malaria-riddled mosquitoes. Her brothers Antoine and Eugenio also came along, one in his infinite wisdom bringing his 10-year-old son so he could go to school in Europe, as well as maids, slaves and a French doctor and his companion seeking an adventure. In the end there would be one survivor – Isabel.

After navigating the Andes, home to active volcanoes, the tired group arrived nine days later at a mission station where they were supposed to retrieve supplies and a boat to travel the Amazon. It was completely empty of life, a true ghost-town that had been ravaged by smallpox before being burnt to the ground by survivors. Sensibly, but unfortunately for Isabel, the porters ran from this hellhole.

Two survivors were found with a rather shoddy boat but the Amazon was not hospitable, and one of the guides drowned when he reached out to grab a hat. The rising waters meant they had to abandon ship leaving them to the mercy of poisonous snakes, wild animals and mosquitoes. Joaquin was sent to look for help.

As they languished, Isabel's young nephew died from infected bites followed quickly by the maids and her brothers. Another maid wandered into the rainforest never to be seen again. As Isabel drifted into a diseased sleep, her companions died around her. When she awoke, probably delirious she cut her brother's shoes off his feet and made them into sandals before attempting to carry on through the jungle.

She was eventually discovered nine days later by some tribal people wandering half-naked save for a ripped shawl or shirt and the sandals. She was delirious and ill and barely knew which way was up. She tried to reward the indigenous rescuers with her gold necklaces but the Christian missionaries took them – another stunning act of mercenary betrayal.

Finally in July 1770 they took her to the ship that had been waiting in Cayenne for years and she came face to face with Jean again. They lived the rest of their lives in France and died within months of each other in 1792, as the greatest lovers so often do.

Isabella of France, Queen of England (1295–1358)

Wow. Where to start. Let's just say that Isabella didn't have an easy time of it.

For daring to stand up for herself, to challenge the status quo, to assert herself and not simply be, as was expected, a wife, mother and queen, she was labelled as a she-wolf. A ravenous, ruthless, rapacious, violent animal. Granted, she did facilitate the murder of her husband in favour of her son. But still. Let's not be picky.

Such name-calling is a systematic pattern in history, repeated for any woman daring to stand up to the status quo. If not labelled a wolf, then perhaps a witch or maybe a whore. Tough choice. (A quick suggestion when learning about Isabella, don't take 'Braveheart' literally.)

Anyhow. Marital bliss is always going to be a challenge when your husband prefers the company of men. As we know from recent royal precedent, three in marriage can make things terribly crowded. Although, to be fair, let's remember that Isabella of France, or Isabella the Fair, was only 12 on 25 January 1308 when she was handed over in a long-standing arranged marriage to the 23-year-old King Edward II of England.

Daughter of Jeanne of Navarre and Philip IV of France, Isabella's wedding in Boulogne was full of pomp and circumstance but it was downhill very quickly after that. Edward decided to favour his lover and knight-of-his-life Piers Gaveston with all his attention. He made him Earl of Cornwall, married him to his own niece to ensure he remained in the royal sphere and, as legend has it, gave him jewellery from Isabella's own wedding dowry.

To compound things even further, Isabella and Edward's coronation was a mess. The newly crowned queen was completely upstaged by Gaveston, who not only carried the coronation crown and made a pig's-ear of organising the event but had his own coat of arms entwined with the king's in the celebratory tapestries. Ouch.

Isabella might have been young, but knew enough to know that she was being usurped. Still, the truth is indeed often stranger than fiction. She remained loyal to her husband. It's not a simple black-and-white case of Isabella hated Edward. The few existing letters between them demonstrate a very real affection, with Isabella calling him 'my very sweet heart' or 'mon tresdoutz coer'.

Edward III, their first child, was born on 13 November 1312. They had three others, John, Eleanor and Joan. Later on in their marriage, after Gaveston had been killed by barons enraged by his arrogant behaviour over the years, from lording it over them to seizing their lands, Edward moved onto a new favourite, Hugh le Depenser the Younger. Hugh made Gaveston look like Mary Poppins in comparison. And a woman can only take so much.

In 1325 Isabella had travelled to France to help secure a peace treaty and settle the conflict between Edward and her brother Charles IV of France. Firmly under Hugh's thumb, Edward had confiscated her lands. Sometime later in that year Isabella decided to stay put in France, with their son, the young Prince of Wales. This was an outrage. But she'd had enough and wasn't going back to England.

Edward II dug his Louboutin heels in and refused to get rid of Dispenser. So Isabella and her lover Roger Mortimer, Baron Wigmore, one of Edward's own generals, took up arms and invaded England, where she had her revenge. Hanged, drawn and quartered, Le Despenser met his grisly and gruesome end on 24 November 1326.

Captured and imprisoned, it was too dangerous for Edward to be left alive. He was murdered at Berkeley Castle in Gloucestershire. Edward was held down and a hot rod forced up his posterior via a cow's horn, essentially burning out all of his internal organs. A calming colonic it was not. (However recent research does suggest that this famous story might not be true, that the murder was faked and Edward escaped.)

Hot rod or not, Isabella installed her teenage son, Edward III, in his father's place, making herself and Mortimer regents until 1330. Ruthlessness clearly ran in the family and the son was smarter than the father; just three years later Edward III executed Mortimer and banished his mother for life.

Dying at the age of 62, Isabella was buried at Greyfriars church in London, wearing the same sumptuous red cloak she had been married in, clasping the casket bearing the heart of the husband and king she had deposed.

Dr James Barry
(1790s–25 July 1865)

Dr James Barry was born in Ireland as Margaret Ann Bulkley, daughter to Mary-Ann and greengrocer Jeremiah. Determined to pursue a medical career, her life changed after her father was imprisoned for debt in 1803. Taken in and helped by her uncle, artist James Barry, whose name she assumed, she lived her life as a man, sailing from London to Edinburgh in 1809 to earn a degree at the city's medical school.

She had the full support of her mother in her endeavour, who took on the charade of 'aunt' to her 'nephew'. Her disguise, only revealed on her death, actually makes Dr James Barry the first woman in Britain to practise medicine, albeit one disguised as a man, perhaps illustrating the extraordinary lengths women were prepared to go to – had to – in order to achieve their ambition.

Dr Barry joined the British army in 1813 and became the Surgeon General, serving in India and South Africa. Not one to rest on her laurels, she was also Inspector-General of Hospitals in Canada, as well as serving in Corfu, the Crimea, Mauritius, Jamaica and St Helena. She was posted to South Africa in 1816, became closely acquainted with its governor Lord Charles Somerset and mysteriously disappeared for a full year, around 1819. This is when some historians believe she gave birth to a presumably stillborn child, before returning to South Africa, where she is credited as being the first British surgeon to perform a Caesarean section in Africa where both mother and child survived the procedure.

Her true gender was uncovered after her death from dysentery on 25 July 1865. Housemaid Sophia Bishop, tasked with preparing the body for burial, disregarded the deceased's last wishes NOT to undress the body and made her startling discovery.

Such was the incredulity at the news that the British army sealed all related records for a century. Whether it was because of the scandal of her fooling the Establishment for so many years or the shock that a mere woman had scaled such incredible career heights, is for you to decide. The likelihood of her having conceived a child was given further weight by the fact that the body bore stretch marks, obviously associated with pregnancy and childbirth.

Dr James fought a duel with pistols, was known to speak her mind and got into a war of words with Florence Nightingale, who later wrote of the altercation:

> I never had such a blackguard rating in all my life – I who have had more than any woman – than from this Barry sitting on his horse, while I was crossing the Hospital Square with only my cap on in the sun. He kept me standing in the midst of quite a crowd of soldiers, Commissariat, servants, camp followers, etc., etc., every one of whom behaved like a gentleman during the scolding I received while he behaved like a brute . . . After he was dead, I was told that (Barry) was a woman . . . I should say that (Barry) was the most hardened creature I ever met.

Rather ironic, considering they were both passionate about health reform in their own way. Dr James also acquiesced to a request from Napoleon to treat the son of his private secretary.

She is buried in Kensal Green Cemetery under the name of James.

Jeanie Cameron of Glendessary, West Highlands (1695?–1773? or 1724?–1786?)

Anyone interested in the alleged lover of Bonnie Prince Charlie, famous for leading the Jacobite rebellions against the English in 1745–6, will discover there are a few Jeanie (or Jennie) Camerons lurking in the pages of history – her story having a nasty case of multiple personality disorder. As the name Jean Cameron is as popular as mince and tatties in Scotland, these mistaken identities are not so surprising.

James Ray, an English historian who followed the Jacobite army in 1745 to their eventual defeat at Culloden, wrote an account of the rebellion. In his work (of fiction?) *A Compleat History of the Rebellion* he waxes lyrical about Jeanie

Jenny Cameron

in a tale so saucy and scandalous it would have made Jackie Collins blush.

It's probable that Mr Ray had been influenced by a Grub Street novel and other tabloid articles. Perhaps, bored by the fighting and bloodshed, the press had leapt upon the news that Miss Cameron had brought 300 Cameron men to support the Jacobites as proof of a scurrilous love affair and shocking behaviour.

James Ray took these stories and gave them the veneer of respectable academia in his history book. Here Jeanie's life is far from boring. Apparently blessed with the look of a slut, what was a girl to do except run wild and engage in several affairs with unsuitable men. Like a Hollywood brat, she was indulged and spoilt by her doting father only to repay him by falling pregnant with a footman's baby. This was either forcibly aborted or miscarried and to prevent the Cameron good name sinking into the Highland bogs, she was told to 'get thee to a nunnery'.

The nuns were no match for her excessive sexual appetite and she was impregnated 'by the Church', and the baby was aborted through the supernatural hands of her dead father. She is then credited with further trysts including an incestuous interlude with her brother that sends his wife to an early grave, before encountering her bonnie prince. A true Scots telenovela.

Following her brother's death, she inherited guardianship of her nephew and his estate. It is she who replaces her nephew to join the king's men. She then brazenly approaches Charles declaring that she was manly enough to fight by his side. If Charles was charmed and delighted by her, he soon forgot her when he fled from Falkirk and she ended up in an Edinburgh dungeon. And it is here the story splits personality. Official records show that a Jean Cameron was indeed caught and interred at the castle's pleasure as evidenced by official records. So when the leader of the English troops, the Duke of Chamberlain, reads a list of prisoners he lends his authority to the idea of the fighting dervish Jeanie Cameron by writing to the Duke of Newcastle proclaiming her capture.

And to ape Chaucer here begins the story of the milliner. Richard Griffith who was also arrested at Stirling claimed this Jean was actually a milliner from Edinburgh, mistakenly identified as the Scarlett Jean. Apparently her time in the dungeon worked out in her favour as all the Edinburgh ladies stampeded her shop when she was released hoping for some scurrilous gossip about the prince. Further stories rose from this phoenix's fire suggesting the milliner's shop was a front for Jacobite espionage. You couldn't make it up . . . oh, wait, yes you could.

And as the Cameron house of cards comes tumbling down further sources claim she was nearly 50, so clearly too old and decrepit for the Young Pretender Charles, and that she never joined his troops at all. No toy boys for Jeanie then.

In most accounts those Jeanies all fell on hard times, reduced to begging and a pauper's death. A more likely version suggests that the real Jeanie Cameron did indeed support the Stuarts and was at that fated Glenfinnan ceremony, but she left and returned home. Rather instead of fighting fiercely at their side, she presented the Jacobites with some cattle to sustain them. She then had to retreat to East Kilbride where she lived out the rest of her days as a respectable and well-bred lady.

Jezebel, Queen of Israel
(9th Century BC)

Calling someone a 'Jezebel' isn't a compliment. Even today the meaning inherent in the name of this Phoenician princess echoes through the ages, denoting wanton, lascivious, man-eating, murdering mayhem. (Although, if you check, there are magazines and perfumes named in her honour.)

Was Jezebel as bad as all that? Or was she written that way as a stark warning to other women to not outstep the traditional, male-dominated bounds of their lives?

Jezebel's notorious story is depicted in the Book of Kings. Married off to King Ahab of Israel as part of a political alliance, it's a fair assumption that she has a reputation of biblical proportions. And in contrast to other women of the Book, she is given a powerful voice. She speaks. She schemes. She raves. She trades insults with her enemies.

She's depicted as a wanton, scheming, heartless seductress and prostitute. And those are just the good points. But women with any sense of independence or sexuality were depicted as such. As were any women who worshipped false gods or idols. Or those who meddled in political affairs – no place for a woman. (They didn't call it the time of the Patriarchs for nothing.) Then there's any biased agenda that the writers of the Bible stories might have had. And there's no mention of her straying sexually from her husband either. That said, without doubt she was ruthless, as tough as nails and had a lot of blood on her hands.

The daughter of King Ethbaal of Tyre, she attempted to wipe out the Jewish religion, murder its priests and install her own faith, worship of Baal, the pagan god of fertility. Upon her marriage to King Ahab she brought with her hundreds of her own priests and attempted to convert her husband. Their idolatrous behaviour proved anathema to the Jewish priest Elijah. He called for a competition between the two gods on Mount Carmel: whichever deity could create fire to destroy a sacrificial bull would be known as the true God. The Jewish monotheistic God won – and Elijah went on to slaughter hundreds of Baal priests. Jezebel is incandescent with rage and threatens to kill him. Elijah, in no uncertain terms, legs it.

Her husband decided he wanted a plot of land adjacent to the royal palace for a garden. The only problem was that it belonged to someone else, a landowner called Naboth, who refused to give it to the king. So the king sulked. He had a proper bottom-lip-quivering, pouty sulk. And Jezebel isn't happy. So she does what any loving wife would in the face of such a crisis; she schemes, forging Ahab's signature on royal proclamations, and has Naboth falsely accused of treason by the people of the village. He is duly stoned to death and Jezebel triumphantly claims the land for Ahab, having stamped down hard on this little episode of rebellion.

Elijah comes back to the story and in true prophetic style, predicts that Jezebel will be ravaged by a pack of wild dogs. In short order, the king dies, their first son follows suit and their second son Joram takes the throne, only to be challenged and murdered by his own military commander Jehu.

Jehu proceeds to pursue Jezebel, intent on killing her too. But she doesn't run. Quite the opposite. She waits at her bedroom window, beautifully dressed, kohl make-up artfully applied to her eyes and her hair adorned. The defiant last act of a queen facing certain death or the panicked actions of a femme fatale desperate to use her feminine charms to change her murderer's mind?

It's a moot point, as her eunuchs throw her out of the window and her body is eaten by wild dogs. Hers is a cautionary tale indeed to other women tempted to follow in her footsteps, rule their husbands or have an opinion that goes against the traditional, monotheistic and patriarchal belief system.

Kalpana Chawla
(1 July 1961–1 February 2003)

Kalpana means 'imagination'; born and raised in Karnal, Haryana, India, Kalpana's story is both inspirational and tragic, of an incredible life of achievement cut short far too soon.

The youngest of four children and the first Indian-born woman in space, Kalpana (KC to her friends) died alongside her six team members on the space shuttle *Columbia* as it exploded on re-entry to earth in 2003. She was only the second Indian person in space.

Passionate about science and space and inspired by India's first pilot, J.R.D. Tata, she completed a course in aeronautical engineering at Punjab Engineering College in Chandigarh, before moving to the US in 1982. What follows is an unbelievable list of academic achievements: a Master of Science degree in Aerospace Engineering from the University of Texas and a doctorate in Aerospace Engineering from the University of Colorado, topped off with a PhD, all before marrying Jean Pierre Harrison in 1988, the same year she started work at NASA. She became a naturalised citizen in April 1991 and joined the NASA Astronaut Corps in March 1995.

In 1997, on board the space shuttle *Columbia*, she was responsible for the Spartan Satellite. Her second and final mission was also on board the STS 107 *Columbia*; the launch was delayed several times before finally taking off in 2003. The crew spent sixteen days in space, conducting scientific research and experiments.

The shuttle was due to land at Kennedy Space Centre on 1 February, but due to a briefcase-sized piece of the wing breaking off at launch it was unable to protect itself from the immense heat of re-entry into the earth's atmosphere. NASA decided against telling the crew of the imminent danger of re-entry. All seven (Commander Rick D. Husband, Pilot William C. McCool, Payload Commander Michael P. Anderson, Payload Specialist Ilan Ramon, the first Israeli astronaut, Mission Specialists David M. Brown and Laurel B. Clark) died as the shuttle de-pressurised and disintegrated over Texas.

Kalpana Chawla was posthumously awarded the Congressional Space Medal of Honor, NASA Space Flight Medal and NASA Distinguished Service Medal. Several academic scholarships have been established in her name, including ones at the International Space University, University of Texas and University of Colorado. There are also asteroids, mountains on Mars, streets, hostels and supercomputers named in her honour.

La Malinche, aka Mallinali, aka Dona Marina (1502–29)

Déjà vu. Mallinali's story is yet another tale of a woman from history that has been retold several times by many different people with many different agendas.

There is only one credible source who actually knew her properly; Bernal Díaz Del Castillo was part of Conquistador Hernan Cortes's party and from his glowing references he may well have had a crush on her. Sadly for Bernal, as Cortes's slave, she was his woman: she literally belonged to him.

Mallinali's mother had sold her into slavery at the age of just 5 years old. The child had inconveniently inherited her aristocratic Aztec father's wealth when he died and Mummy Dearest wanted her son from her new husband to get the loot. So she pretended Mallinali had died. The girl was passed around between various owners and details from this part of her life are hard to find. One can surmise she didn't have too many options, which makes judgmental historical interpretations of her all the more galling.

Mallinali's name was first vilified after Mexico won independence from Spain and the country was riding a wave of hatred against the name Hernan Cortes and all associated with him. In their versions, Cortes had arrived on indigenous lands with only a small number of men to defeat the mighty Aztecs. By this time he clearly wasn't the god he had first been mistaken for so how did he do it? Obviously his temptress lover Mallinali was a traitor and helped him massacre thousands of innocent Indians. Cortes didn't help matters by citing her as the reason for winning New Spain.

The truth of course was a great deal more complicated. In recent years feminists have come to Mallinali's rescue and pointed out that the girl had little choice but to do as she was told after being sold to the Spanish Conquistador, whether that be sleeping with Cortes or interpreting tribal leaders (it was her great skill in indigenous languages that originally rocked his boat) and negotiating alliances with the Spanish. For that is what they were, alliances and not always conquered victims.

At that time Mexico was not composed of one uniformed Aztec community but of several rival tribes who all hated each other. Many of these tribes especially hated Montezuma, King of the Aztecs, whose repeated calls for human sacrifice and cruelty weren't a crowd pleaser. So it didn't take a huge amount of persuasion to get them singing 'Kumbaya' with the Spanish.

Modern interpretations claim that Mallinali probably saved many more lives by negotiating treaties with Cortes rather than constant warfare. It also seems rather unfair to blame her for the decimation of the Aztec capital Tenochtitlan, which was actually ravaged by smallpox and not a teenage girl. Mallinali became the scapegoat for a country constantly worried about its own identity. Was it Spanish, indigenous or too much a mix of the two? Was the Spanish invasion a blessing that rid them of the fierce Montezuma or a scourge of indigenous life?

Mallinali had a son by Cortes, the first recorded *mestizo* (child of mixed descent) in Mexican history. There would have been many more babies of mixed Spanish and indigenous blood but none of their stories were recorded. On the other side of the spectrum, many people have romanticised her life, waxing lyrical on the great love she and Cortes had, although ultimately he went back to his more suitable wife.

There is endless debate as to whether la Malinche was the mother to or traitor of the Mexican people. Each different political and cultural group interpreted her story to suit their particular bias and her name has become deeply entwined with the country's identity crisis.

Lili Elbe (1882–1931) and Gerda Gottlieb (1885–1940)

Transsexual, LGBT and intersexual are today's big buzzwords and a culture is emerging that finally welcomes this community. But what of those men and women born in the wrong body who lived in eras when gender definitions were utterly rigid and uncompromising?

Artist Lili Elbe was born Einar Magnus Andreas Wegene. Einar met Gerda Gottlieb at the Royal Danish Academy of Fine Arts and they married, living as a heterosexual couple. Both were talented but Elbe's landscapes were more successful in Denmark than Gerda's Art Deco work. Her risqué depictions of nudity, eroticism and women actually enjoying themselves sexually were too much for the delicate sensibilities of Copenhagen. When they discovered that her delicate and pretty artist's model was actually her husband, smelling salts must have sold out.

Einar was eager to help his wife's career and the couple moved to Paris in 1912, a city far more bohemian and receptive to her scandalous exhibitions, but less enamoured by his landscapes. Gerda was hugely successful as an illustrator for some of France's greatest magazines. More importantly she was a pioneering beacon for women in the art world, depicting women as the subject of a painting rather than as the object of our gaze. Plus she loved to imbue her work with a sense of cheek and sass.

France's avant-garde capital was also a haven for Einar. After he reluctantly stepped quite literally into the stockings of his wife's model who had to cancel, Einar awoke his alter ego Lili. He discovered how comfortable he felt in women's clothes and modelled more and more for Gerta. By all accounts she loved Lili and when a little bored would ask Einar to let Lili come out and play. By moving to Paris there was more anonymity and freedom for him to visit parties, carnivals and artist soirées as a woman. Gerta would introduce him as Elbe, Einar's sister. Only their closest friends knew the truth.

Was Gerda a lesbian as many people seem to suggest? Maybe she was, maybe she was bi and maybe she was just spicing up their sex life as well as showing support for his transformation. Her paintings gave Lili a space to launch her identity. However, as Einar felt more and more comfortable as Lili, she became more despondent at her situation. She felt very deeply that internally she must be female and when she started to experience nose bleeds every month Lili believed they were a manifestation of the periods she should be having. Doctors dismissed her as either unbalanced or a homosexual. Some even diagnosed schizophrenia. It was a terrible time, and a desolate Lili describes feeling being torn between two people. Driven to despair she marked the start of spring, 1 May 1930 as the date she would commit suicide.

A friend introduced her to German specialists Magnus Hirschfield and Kurt Warnekros in Dresden, who apparently confirmed the presence of undeveloped ovaries in her abdomen.

In Lili's autobiography, her relief at finally being taken seriously is heartbreakingly tangible. With the sale of her artwork and financial and emotional support from Gerda and her brother-in-law she was able to pay for surgeries to remove her penis and scrotum as well as experimental procedures to add a uterus and vagina.

Whilst she felt her truest self during this time, it was a painful period. She was rejected by many of her male friends and felt she had murdered Einar. She was no longer able to paint. Art had been Einar's occupation. They returned to Denmark where she intended to live as Lili but someone leaked her story to the press leading to public derision and disgust. So she took the matter in her own hands and told her story herself.

The Danish authorities issued a new passport in the name of Lili Elbe and the King of Denmark effectively annulled their marriage. Two women were not allowed to be married. By now she had fallen in love with an art dealer called Claude Lejaune and was hoping that surgery would complete her as a woman able to have full sex and become a mother.

Tragically it was not to be and she died from heart complications following the surgery, probably from a rejection of the transplanted organ.

Gerda was devastated by her death and life was not kind to her in the years that followed. She married an Italian officer Fernando Porta but divorced a short time later and after he had gone through all her money. She was broke, her artistic style fell from fashion and she had to make postcards to earn a living. She ended up drinking and living in poverty and obscurity.

Lili's story has helped blur the rigid definitions of sexuality and gender identification but she could never have done this without the unquestioning love and support of Gerda. Lili and Gerda were both remarkable women whose unselfish sisterly love for each other was heroic in itself.

Lilith
(A Long Time Ago In a Garden Far, Far Away)

If you want some drama in your life then there's nothing like the Creation story to stir up emotions between religious creationists and Dawkins evolutionary enthusiasts.

Just mention Adam and Eve, sit back and watch the sparks fly. Yet some of the earlier interpretations of the Garden of Eden also mention another woman, one who seems to have been forgotten, perhaps deliberately. For she represents a dangerous symbol to a patriarchal society so fiercely protected by our medieval authors.

Enter Lilith, the first woman created by God at the same time as Adam and from the same earth. Lilith is the first feminist to walk this earth, if you don't

count Ms Neanderthal (see Lucy). From the start she demands equality with Adam. And Adam doesn't like it – never mind original sin, he is the original cliché. Lilith is first mentioned in ancient Mesopotamian texts where she is represented as a demon.

These Creation stories were copied into two versions at some point, one mentions Lilith and the other does not. In a satirical interpretation penned anonymously in the text Alphabet of Sirach, the story of Lilith is written as a bawdy and hilarious text alongside many anecdotes about farts and other forms of puerile humour. In this version, she is a woman with insatiable sexual demands. If she wants sex she isn't about to sit making pretty moon eyes and rearranging her lotus leaves until Adam takes the hint. She asks for it and she wants satisfaction god damn it. Lilith prefers sex on top, which according to this interpretation means that she wants to take power; it's nothing to do with the position of the G-spot, it's all about controlling men. By now Adam, due to some design flaw perhaps, is feeling emasculated and determined to exert power over her by claiming that as a subordinate she should lay beneath him. Cue the world's first relationship row.

In the end Lilith leaves the Garden of Eden, whether by force or her own free will depends on which version you read. Adam then asks God for an 'easier' woman, perhaps one that will give his poor old battered balls a rest. And so Eve is born from his rib, eager to please and obey, until she is seduced by the wily serpent, who some people believe is Lilith in another form.

Our medieval brothers would have it that when Lilith leaves the garden she becomes a demon threatening death, destruction and general evil misdoings, including persuading the pious Eve to eat the apple and so set off a chain of catastrophic events for the rest of eternity. This idea was lent credence by Michaelangelo who painted her as a half-serpent, half-woman coiled around the Tree of Knowledge.

Many of the Lilith myths (of which there are many and none of them complimentary) depict her as a baby-eating demon preying upon pregnant women and new born babes. Holding a demon goddess responsible during eras of high infant mortality gave people a target for their fear and blame. Unfortunately it also set up horrific stereotypes of women.

Luckily some women have reinterpreted this story and added their own twist, casting Lilith as a biblical suffragette. To them she represents freedom and equality, and is, one might say, one of the first to demand education for woman in the form of the apple from the Tree of Life. And she shares this knowledge in a sisterly relationship with Eve when they meet beyond the walls of the garden.

Whether you believe in creationism or evolution is incidental; Lilith's story has severe repercussions for thousands of years that still reverberate today. Hers is one of the first tales to set up the dangerous dynamic of angel versus whore, mother versus monster. It's a dynamic repeated throughout history to polarise women into two impossible states of being, and deny them that which really makes us human – a complex personality possessing good, bad and everything in between.

Lucrezia Borgia
(18 April 1480–24 June 1519)

The background: Italy isn't unified but is instead a collection of warring papal states, duchies, kingdoms and republics.

The scene: Renaissance Italy. Corruption. Incest. Extravagance. Excess. Poison. Sex. Seduction. Privilege. Ruthless political intrigue. Illegitimate children. Depravity. Blackmail. Bribery. Nepotism. (And that was just on a quiet day.)

This is the tale of a fifteenth-century Italian woman born into the real-deal of a crime family, a woman whose name continues to spark controversy and interest long after her death. Was she an

innocent pawn, used ruthlessly by her social climbing, politically ambitious family? A family whose escapades would make life at the 'Sopranos' house look like afternoon tea at a convent? Or was she a willing participant in their scurrilous schemes and plotting, a cold-hearted poisoner of rivals, a heartless harlot? The truth may be somewhere in between.

The beautiful Lucrezia was the illegitimate daughter of Pope Alexander VI, Rodrigo Borgia and his long-term mistress Vannozza dei Cattanei, who also provided siblings in the form of Cesare Borgia, Giovanni Borgia and Gioffre Borgia. Lucrezia wasn't brought up by her mother, instead living in the household of Adriana daMila, a cousin of her father.

Engaged twice before the age of 12, Lucrezia's first political marriage of alliance was to Giovanni Sforza, Lord of Pesaro in 1493. Fifteen years older than Lucrezia, poor Giovanni was urged to bed his wife in front of the Borgias and his own family in order to prove his manhood. In 1497, when the relationship was no longer politically expedient for the Borgia family, the marriage was annulled on the basis of non-consummation.

However someone definitely consummated something because Lucrezia, sent to a convent during the annulment, had an illegitimate son called Giovanni, hidden from public view until he was 3.

Italian society went into overdrive, taking wild guesses at the paternity of the child. Rumours of incest raged, not helped by the Papal Bulls issued on the matter, the first stating Giovanni's father as Cesare, Lucrezia's brother, the second Bull then awarding paternity to her own father, Rodrigo. The likely actual father, Pedro Perotto Calderon, a servant in Pope Alexander's household, was found drowned in the River Tiber.

Lucrezia's second marriage in 1498, also for her family's political gain, was to Alfonso V of Aragon, Prince of Naples and Duke of Bisceglie. That liaison didn't end so well either; brother Cesare strangled him.

There were also the feverish whispers of Lucrezia's adroitness at poisoning enemies (she allegedly had her own bespoke ring to store the stuff), and her scandalous involvement in events of legendary sexual excess, such as the Banquet of the Chestnuts on 30 October 1501, an orgy at the Palace of Rome for nobles and senior members of the Catholic Church, complete with courtesans and prostitutes, all organised (naturally) by the Borgia family.

Marriage number three occurred in 1502, this time to Afonse d'Este, Prince of Ferrarra. This was a case of third-time lucky; although they both had affairs, it was a happy marriage producing four children.

Pope Alexander would die in 1503, providing some respite for Lucrezia from her family's all-consuming political machinations. When Afonse's father died, he and Lucrezia would become the Duke and Duchess of Ferrara. She would turn to patronage of the arts and religion in the latter years of her life.

Lucrezia died at the age of 39 from pureperal fever following the birth of a daughter, who also died. She is buried in the convent of Corpus Domini.

Lucy, or AL 288-1

In 1974, in the extreme heat of the Ethiopian desert, weary palaeontologists Donald Johanson and his colleague Tom Gray took a detour back to camp after a long, hot day sifting through sand.

It was then, in the dust of an ancient lake bed in the area of Hadar, that Donald discovered a fragment of elbow bone, swiftly followed by other bones including a bit of skull. Clutching bits of fossilised bone in sweaty hands may not be everyone's idea of a fabulous afternoon but to Donald and his team it was like winning the lottery. For the first time they had found the most complete set of remains of a single hominid. In total 40 per cent of a skeleton, the team were confident that their find, named AL 288-1, came from one female.

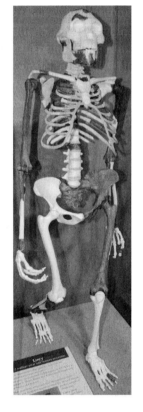

They took the party back to camp where they celebrated all night long to an endless repeat of the Beatles classic homage to drugs 'Lucy in the Sky with Diamonds'. Possibly slightly the worse for wear, a canny member of the team suggested naming AL 288-1 'Lucy'.

A mere 3 million and a bit years old, Lucy was the first almost complete skeleton ever found, a crucial piece of the evolutionary jigsaw that scientists today are still trying to put together. She is yet another possible contender for the title 'the first woman on earth'. From the creationists to the Darwinists there is a first lady for everyone. And she adds to the evidence that humans originated from Africa. However in this case we can't blame sexism for our knowing so little about Lucy's life, thoughts or motives. Forty bits of skeleton help paint a picture but they cannot conjure up a fully illustrated autobiographical diary from a hominid species with a brain that was closer to Bubbles the Chimpanzee's than Jane Austen.

According to science bods it wasn't her brain, but the fact that she walked on two legs that make her a likely candidate for our great, great (to the power of some really big number) grandmother. Her knees and pelvis point to her walking on two legs whilst other skeletal parts such as long, muscular arms tell us she spent a great deal of her time in trees.

Lucy has proven to be a rather famous globetrotter, in demand across the world. Everyone literally wants a piece of her but her pieces are a very delicate so many museums refuse to exhibit her out of serious concern it would all be a bit much for the old gal.

Controversy also surrounds her death. (Where is CSI Ethiopia when you need it?) In 2008 whilst on a tour of the US, she was secretly examined at the University of Texas whilst being exhibited at the Houston Museum of Natural Science. Using some swanky new technology, a group called Team Lucy was able to examine her bones in depth, revealing several tiny fractures consistent with a fall from a great height. Was she pushed by a jealous hominid because she had prettier and longer arms? Apparently she was about 3.5ft tall and approximately 60lb. However, no matter which designer you might dress her in she would still have looked far more like one of our hairier ape cousins than a Victoria Secrets girl.

Newer discoveries made since Lucy even question whether she indeed was one of our ancient ancestors. She is still studied today and represents an important part of an evolutionary mystery that remains to be fully unravelled.

Footnote: Hominids refer to the evolutionary line that possibly leads to humans. It is known that this evolutionary process was a rather messy mix of various hominids and not a simple straight line.

Luisa Casati
(1881–1957)

Luisa Casati, an Italian heiress, socialite and muse, wowed and scandalised society in the first half of the twentieth century. But would she be considered so avant-garde today?

She wanted to be a living piece of art. The twenty-first century is knee-deep in artists vying to be controversial, many of whom are probably influenced by Luisa. Next to unmade beds in Turner competitions, cows sliced in half and a massive pair of butt cheeks cupped by a pair of hands, our generation would barely raise an eyebrow.

However, her era was still recovering from the shock of seeing women's bare legs, so she had a captive audience. What was more outrageous was her decadent and hugely wasteful lifestyle, a contrived insanity that included: taking pet cheetahs for walkies, chivvied along by their diamond leads whilst she strolled naked in her furs (quite literally all fur coat and no knickers); booking a room at the Paris Ritz for herself and her pet boa constrictor (in case she needed a hug); adorning her naked staff in gold leaf and wearing live snakes as necklaces. At least she never ran the risk of bumping into someone wearing the same outfit.

Luisa was born in 1881 to well-heeled and extremely wealthy parents. By the 1930s, she would have frittered away every last penny of their immense fortune and accumulated eye-watering debt in her quest to be immortalised as an original piece of art. Poverty didn't stop her obsessive desire to stand out from the crowd, as she raided bins outside theatres to find accessories, some of them made out of newspaper. Perhaps she really was the bohemian incarnate, living for art and art alone? Certainly she could use her distaste for bourgeois conventions as an excuse for cuckolding her husband to play lover and muse for the controversial and womanising poet Gabrielle d'Annunzio.

Tall, thin and eager to shock, she made an inspiring coat hanger for noted designers including Leon Bakist and Mariano Fortuny, all of them delighted to let their imaginations run riot over her body. She was particularly famous for short fiery red hair (dyed), very pale white skin, heavy black kohl and green eyes made to look large and luscious by squirting highly toxic belladonna in her eyes. She was quite the Edwardian Goth. In her bid to be unique and visually entertaining, she changed her look as many times as her and her artists' imaginations would allow and paraded herself as a live piece of installation art through the opulent party season that was the 1920s.

Her parties were legendary, the stuff of Gatsby dreams, or nightmares, depending on your perspective. They were attended by the great and the not so good, such as the radical dancer Isadora Duncan, Picasso and several wax figures who joined guests for dinner. At these extravaganzas Luisa would emerge as a living sculpture adorned in fabulous clothes, such as a creation made from her own albino peacocks' feathers accessorised with chicken blood.

Desperate for immortality, she also blew her fortune being a patron, and often lover, for emerging artists as long as they found new and more decadent ways to exhibit her. She was art's greatest Narcissus. One of her many homes housed an art gallery filled with over a hundred images of her.

People may condemn her as a frivolous socialite, yet her hedonistic, idiosyncratic personality drew the art world to her. She inspired artists, poets, writers, sculptors, designers and Hollywood film stars, including Giovanni Boldini and Cecil Beaton, not to mention the Cartier panther collection. She lit the creative lights of geniuses across the artistic spectrum, including surrealism, Dadaism and even artists from the Fauve movement.

She may have spent her final years in poverty, but those who loved her made sure she was buried in style with false eyelashes and her favourite stuffed Pekinese dog. For all her faults, she was totally indifferent to public opinion and defiantly her own woman.

Madame du Barry
(19 August 1743–8 December 1793)

Diamonds aren't always a girl's best friend. And in the case of low-born Marie-Jeanne Becu, Comtesse du Barry and the final Maîtresse-en-Titre (Chief Mistress) to King Louis XV of France, they would prove fatal.

The illegitimate daughter of a seamstress and a friar, a sometime milliner's assistant and hairdresser, the young and beautiful convent-educated Jeanne caught the eye of high-class pimp Jean-Baptiste du Barry, who first made her his mistress, then sold her off to the highest bidders in Parisian society as an expensive courtesan. She proved immensely popular and one can only imagine the names in her little black book of clients.

From there, it was only a matter of time before she caught the attention of the ageing King of France, desolate since the death of his previous Maîtresse-en-Titre, Madame de Pompadour. However the only way for her to gain entry to the upper echelons of court society was to have a title; in 1768, Louis XV swiftly married her off to Jean-Baptiste's brother Guillaume, who was then paid handsomely to make himself scarce. To the disgust and dismay of the royal court, the king then installed the newly ennobled 'Madame du Barry' in private apartments. After bribing an impoverished court 'sponsor', he had her officially presented to the court at Versailles. She would be Maîtresse-en-Titre from 1769–74.

Madame wasn't interested in politics, choosing instead to be a generous patron of the arts whilst also spending vast amounts on exquisite clothes and jewellery for herself. By all accounts she was a generous, good-hearted woman who never forgot her friends, petitioning the king herself on their behalf when they found themselves in dire straits. The king adored her and indulged her hugely extravagant lifestyle and helped alleviate her large debts – a lifestyle that would not help her cause as the Revolution loomed.

Marie Antoinette, the Dauphine and wife of the king's grandson, together with the king's own daughters, turned up their noses at Madame du Barry, viewing her as a morally repugnant street-level upstart. Marie Antoinette rarely acknowledged her at court and only after extreme pressure from her mother, the Archduchess of Austria, to show diplomatic tact, stiffly and reluctantly remarked to her, 'There are many people at Versailles today.' As the French court used the rules of don't speak to royalty until you are spoken to, this finally legitimised du Barry, although she was far from accepted by it.

By this time the Comtesse had been given a 'manners makeover' and was an elegant member of the royal court. When she wasn't there, she would retire to the lands given to her by the king, estates near Louveciennes. After the death of the king in May 1774, Madame du Barry was banished to a convent, before retiring to enjoy years of luxury at the chateau and estates she shared with the Duke of Brissac, from where she made several trips to London.

In January 1791 she returned home to discover she had been robbed and a huge amount of jewellery stolen. Publishing a long list of the missing jewellery with an offer of a huge reward was the worst thing she could have done. It called attention to herself, the spendthrift, extravagant mistress of the King of France, at a time when the Revolution was looking increasingly likely.

Historians differ in opinion on what followed. She did travel back and forth to London four times. Some researchers believe that whilst ostensibly this was on the pretext of working to rescue her jewellery, she was however likely a counter-revolutionary using these journeys to smuggle counter-Revolutionary émigrés and her own fortune out of France. Other academics insist on her innocence and political naivety. Either way, she proved too big a scalp for the Revolutionaries to pass on; with the explosion of the French Revolution in 1792, she was duly captured and imprisoned on one of her return visits home.

In a desperate bid to save her life, she provided her captors with a full list of all her jewellery and where to find it; the attempt failed. The Revolutionaries gladly took the list and sent the 50-year-old du Barry to meet the brutal blade of Madame La Guillotine on 8 December 1793 in the Place de la Revolution.

Not for her the calm, dignified resigned silence of others who shared her fate. She went to her death kicking, screaming, crying and begging for mercy. But to no avail. Her final words to the executioner were: 'Encore un moment, monsieur le bourreau, un petit moment.' ('One moment more, executioner, one little moment.')

In a bizarre twist to her tale, du Barry is the name given to French foods served with cauliflower, perhaps in a homage to her wigs or curvy figure, including the garnish 'à la Dubarry', Eggs du Barry, Cocktail du Barry and Crème Madame du Barry (cauliflower soup).

Madam Sacho
(18th Century)

So where are the Iroquois (or the Haudenosaunee to use their preferred name)? What did they have to say? What did the women have to say?

Unfortunately the scant stories that exist are mostly written from the colonists's perspective. It is difficult to hear the Haudenosaunee women, including Madam Sacho, who illuminated a particularly dark episode in the colonisation of Native America and Canada.

During the American Revolution under the leadership of the much-revered (slave-owning) George Washington there had been a slew of violent, brutal skirmishes between the colonists and the Iroquois. In addition many Native Americans had chosen to help the British and were proving to be a tenacious

threat to the luscious green pastures of the brand new American dream. The colonists' response, known as 'Sullivan's Campaign', was ruthless, cruel and wantonly destructive. The campaign may have been spearheaded by Major General John Sullivan, but it was given the go-ahead by Washington.

Of course the situation was not black and white or indeed red, white and blue. It was a bitter campaign fought between desperate people and fear doesn't lend itself to flowers and trust circles. It followed a series of bitter raids during which the Native Americans had pitilessly ravaged settlements killing men, women and children.

Fear was very much at the heart of this devastating strategy. Washington's men were ordered to raze every Iroquois settlement to the ground, to kill the men, burn the crops and carry off women and children in the hope that they would run away or be cowed into submission. Although most fled, it was an unrelenting destruction of crop pastures that the colonists were hoping to farm themselves.

It was in an abandoned settlement that an old, wizened woman appeared before a group of soldiers. She was alone in a village that was the Native American version of the *Mary Celeste*, utterly deserted, kettles hanging above fire pits and life set to pause. Some men wanted to kill her but respect for her age and gender prevailed. With the help of an Oneida interpreter, she told the troops that her village had held a council in which the men said they must flee, although some women wanted to stay and guard the crops but in the end they left. She told the soldiers that the women had gone towards Seneca Lake. None of this answered why she was there alone but the men left her with food and shelter despite being low on rations themselves – perhaps burning those crops wasn't the smartest idea.

Why was she there? Perhaps she planned to misdirect the soldiers to a false location whilst her people sought safety in a different direction. Certainly, she told them that many of the women had gone towards Seneca Lake and almost 400 men went searching to no avail. Thanks to a limited patriarchal imbued imagination, the men would have failed to credit some 'poor old dear' with the influence and nous to stay and misdirect the army, if that was her reason. The colonists failed to realise that Iroquios women were an important voice in society, instrumental in decision-making and agriculture.

When they returned to the village they found Madam Sacho still there but they also discovered the corpse of a young Native American girl who had been shot. A depressing tragedy in every way and a young girl whose name will never be known, her story never told, her death never given justice. We don't even know Madam Sacho's real name, it was simply one of the kinder names she was given by the soldiers. We searched in vain for the Haudenosaunee's take on this story but couldn't find it, although that's not to say it doesn't exist but it's certainly not readily available.

Madam Stephanie Queen St Clair
(1880s?–1969)

Prohibition Harlem knew her as Madam St Clair, whilst Manhattan referred to her as 'Queenie'. The legendary Lady Gangster of Harlem dressed accordingly, and was known for being elegant and sophisticated but with the mouth of a fishwife.

Madam said she was born in France. But let's take everything Madam said with a very large pinch of salt. Evidence suggests she was actually from Guadeloupe. Likely born in the 1880s, she probably arrived in New York's Harlem via Marseille by steamer in 1911 or 1912, when she may have been in her early 20s. No one knew her actual age and Madam sure as hell wasn't going to tell anyone.

She started her criminal career as a leader of local extortion gang the 40 Thieves, effectively the first black syndicate in US history. Her right-hand man was arguably the first black gangster, Ellsworth 'Bumpy' Johnson (so-called because of a large bump on the back of his head). She also allied with legendary mobster Lucky Luciano to keep other hoods out of her territory.

Clearly educated, she spoke French, Spanish and English and could probably express extreme profanities in all three. She was that rare thing: a female gangster in a strictly white, male gangster world, living up on Sugar Hill, the place to live in Harlem. She started off her numbers business with $10,000; rumours abound on how a penniless woman from Guadeloupe got her hands on that sort of money. To put it in context, President Hoover was on around $30,000 a year.

By the 1920s she was known as the 'Numbers Queen of Harlem', 'numbers' referring to the illegal lottery that residents of Harlem played, usually for a penny but the game was worth millions. She was soon a black, female gangster millionaire.

In 1928 Queenie's rival Casper Holstein was ambushed and held to ransom for $50,000, upon receipt of which he was released. Rumour has it that notorious Bronx gangster Dutch Schultz was behind it. A Jewish bootlegger, known as the 'Beer Baron of the Bronx' as the Great Depression deepened and the end of Prohibition neared, he needed to diversify his business interests and wanted in on the Harlem numbers game.

But the black gangsters in Harlem, including Madam, didn't want any white gangsters encroaching on their territory. Things got violent with around forty people murdered, including many Harlem numbers operators. Schultz sent assassins to take Madam out; she evaded them, hid under the bed and survived the attempt, but held one hell of a grudge. In 1935, when Schultz lay dying from a multiple gunshot wounds (allegedly 'taken out' by Lucky Luciano), she sent a telegram to his hospital bed simply staying: 'As ye sow, so shall ye reap.'

Both adored and feared by the Harlem community, she fought fiercely as an activist for civil rights, providing jobs and fighting against racism, exposing police brutality and corruption by placing advertisements in newspapers blatantly talking about the bribes she'd given them. Her actions led to the arrest of several police officers.

She shot her own husband, alleged cult leader Sufi Abdul Hamid, for purportedly cheating on her, later claiming that the gun went off by accident. Hamid was a real piece of work; he claimed to be a descendant of Egyptian pharaohs, was an anti-Semite, known as Black Hitler and was convicted of stabbing a communist organiser in 1936.

For shooting him, Madam was sentenced to ten years in New York State Prison for Women, for first-degree assault and possession of a concealed weapon – it's unclear how many she actually served. Sufi divorced her, later dying in a plane crash which he piloted himself.

Queenie turned over the business to Bumpy in the 1940s and focused her efforts on civil rights before disappearing from view to die in her early 70s in 1969.

Madeleine de Verchères
(1678–1747)

At first glance Madeleine de Verchères, at the tender age of 14, is one seriously hardcore heroine. However, her story is not all it seems and for once that's not just the result of some misogynist historians, it's also thanks to her own exaggerated retelling of the incident that turned her into a French Canadian icon.

She may be better described as a smart and savvy operator. What is interesting is why she embellished her tale and why French Canada needed her so badly as a symbol of #independence, #sisterhood, #canadianhero.

There are two accounts of the Iroquois raid of 1692 in letters Madeleine wrote; the first in 1699 as part of an appeal for a pension; and the latter written in 1722 to the king several years after the event. The second letter was a far more intrepid tale of derring-do than the former. Did she even write these letters or were they penned by a couple of over-excited contemporary authors (La Potherie and Charlevoix) who persuaded Madeleine that a more heroic version would secure her and her family a much-needed pension? She may have exaggerated the truth but other reports of the raid do not mention Madeleine at all.

So what was this intrepid tale that earned her the accolade 'Canadian Joan of Arc'? It all began in the cabbage fields outside Fort Verchères, the seigneury of Madeleine's father. Her parents had been called away on business leaving their 14-year-old daughter in charge of her siblings and the fort.

All was peaceful whilst Madeleine and about twenty of the settlers tended their crops, blissfully unaware of the Iroquois warriors hidden in the undergrowth. They had been waiting silently biding their time to attack and it was a huge shock when they pounced, capturing twenty settlers. Madeleine escaped by slipping free of her kerchief that the Iroquois had seized. She ran full pelt to the fort.

In the first letter she was very close to the fort, in the second she had to run much further as forty-five 'savages' fired at her. She ran to the fort calling 'aux armes, aux armes', climbed the bastion and quickly put on a soldier's hat. She then fired the canon to alert her neighbours and to give the Iroquois the impression that the fort was well manned. She encouraged the others, who apparently were useless cowards, to make as much noise as possible to fool the natives. This takes a day or two at the most in her first version, and in the later one it takes a full week before the Iroquois end their siege and head for the hills. The French army arrive to relieve the situation. At which point Madeleine dramatically surrenders her arms to the strong hands of the lieutenant so she can go back to being a proper young lady. This was an important addition to the tale as it allowed the settlers and future generations of chauvinist French Canadians to celebrate a national hero but not one that challenges their male dominance – a heroine who knows her place. The second account added further embellishments such as rescuing two visitors by canoe, but the longer version can be saved for an exciting bedside story.

Why did she write these letters, especially the second? Probably money was a strong motive and frankly who can blame her? There were few ways for a woman to earn a crust in the seventeenth century. And she knew just how far to take her heroic deeds making sure to let people know she only acted in a 'manly' fashion out of necessity.

But what of the shadowy Iroquois in this narrative? They are nothing more than nameless hostile barbarians making the morally upright settlers's lives difficult. Perhaps it's time to hear from the Iroquois women (see Madam Sacho).

Marie Antoinette
(1755–93)

If you ask the average person on the street what they know about Queen Marie Antoinette, it's very likely they'll utter that well-worn cliché 'Let them eat cake'. And yet she never said it. Not once. Not ever. Many women were accused of saying it by various misogynists long before Marie was even born. She wasn't perfect but the scandals and rumours that dogged her reign successfully painted an enduring picture of a degenerate, unfeeling spendthrift. Her courage, philanthropy and maternal skills have gone by largely unnoticed.

It didn't help that Marie had been woefully unprepared for court

and its intimidating, intellectually snobby courtiers. One of many children, she was never expected to marry a future king and consequently her education had been neglected. She was nearly illiterate by the time she became the most viable daughter to marry French royalty, leaving her insecure around the intellectual elite at Versailles.

Her husband King Louis XVI was a chubby, bookish teenager who was suddenly crowned king after his much-lauded brother died. He and Marie were thrust unprepared onto a glittering, gilded and opulent Versailles throne and court. Just slightly intimidating, it's no wonder the lad couldn't perform on his wedding night. It actually took seven years to do the deed.

It's true that Ms Antoinette loved her retail therapy but the Versailles court had embraced an excessive culture of extravagance long before she became Dauphine. And lest we forget, she was only 14 years old when she married Louis. She was literally a teenage girl let loose with an unimaginable income in a candy land of extravagant dresses, lavish parties and big hair that would put the 1980s to shame.

Far costlier to France were the battles Marie endorsed, in particular the American Revolution, which emptied the royal coffers faster than you could say Madame Deficit (the not so affectionate nickname hurled her way). And yet there are several anecdotes that show her to be empathetic and generous, including the time she stopped her carriage to help an injured peasant, refusing to leave until the doctor she called arrived. Nonetheless, the starving, beleaguered population of France needed a scapegoat, amply promoted by thousands of illegal pamphlets printed by her enemies. These accused the queen of various scandals from sexual deviance to blaming her for a famous diamond fraud. In the French imagination she was transformed from a sweet and inexperienced teen queen to a dissolute monster bleeding the country dry.

She was a contradiction, supporting the American Revolution yet raised to mix with all social classes. She believed passionately in the Divine Right of Kings – a deadly conviction to cling to in the French Revolution. She refused to accede to the new government, plotted to run away and encouraged war with Austria in a bid to regain the throne. Robespierre must have rubbed his hands in glee at the woeful mismanagement of the situation.

Daughter of an Austrian emperor, Marie Antoinette was already on shaky ground as the French and Austrians had a chequered relationship. The royal court questioned whether her loyalties were to France or Austria. From there, it was but a hop, skip and a mob-fuelled jump to being convicted of treason, with some incest thrown in too from her young son's forced testimony (kangaroo anyone).

Her final days showed the strength of her character. Gone was the frivolous, spendthrift teenager and in its stead stood a courageous and resolute mother, protecting her brood and standing by her man. Her final sob-stained letter to her sister asked that her children not take revenge. And she approached the guillotine with her hair shorn wearing a shabby shift and with her head held high, until it was chopped off of course.

Marie was painted into history as the symbol of all that was wrong with noble rule. As we unravel the lies from the truth and discover a human being replete with foibles, faults and amazing strengths too, let those propagandists eat humble pie.

Marie Marvingt
(1875–1963)

Marie Marvingt was such an astonishing sportswoman, combat pilot, inventor and nurse, such a veritable Olympian, you'd be forgiven for thinking she was an actual daughter of the gods of Olympus. She won prizes in swimming, fencing, shooting, ski jumping, skating and so on and on and on. She was the first woman to climb most of the Swiss and French Alps; to ride the course of the Tour de France but not during the actual race (women weren't allowed); to swim the River Seine; to fly a hot air balloon across the North Sea and English Channel. In fact it would be quicker to list what she did not excel at.

So instead we will progress to her other firsts – first woman to fly a combat mission and to be certified as a flight nurse. Oh and lest we forget, she also invented a new type of surgical suture. She won enough medals, declarations and acclamations to decorate a thousand toilets. Superwoman – it's time to give up your crown. In her spare time she wrote prize-winning poetry. Now be honest, hands up who hates her?

Whilst Marie clearly lived life to the fullest, her *raison d'être* was to create medical air ambulances. Marie had the idea in 1910 when air travel was in its infancy. It was also at its most dangerous – a thrill she enjoyed, but not one that people wanted to risk as a rescue venture. Nonetheless, she designed a prototype air ambulance with Louis Bechereau, an aviation engineer. She raised the money for this prototype to be built by the Deperdussin factory, but its owner embezzled funds in 1913 scuppering her aircraft. Undeterred, Marie, the stiff upper lip champion, just kept campaigning.

During the First World War, our intrepid Marie continued to impress – we would expect nothing less. Initially she disguised herself as a soldier and went to the front lines but she was discovered. She wasn't home long before she was asked to take supplies to soldiers in the remote Dolomite Mountains using her superior skiing skills. During this time she also trained as a nurse and served as a volunteer pilot engaging in an aerial bombardment. But her air ambulance proposals were still ignored.

After the war there was renewed interest in the idea of aviation rescue, and Marie worked like a dog to publicise the idea, raise funds and attended literally thousands of conferences and meetings for aviation and medical hob-nobs. Finally in 1934 the French government asked her to set up an air ambulance service in Morocco, for which she was – wait for it – awarded another medal. She then turned her hand to training the personnel that would man the aircraft. She never stopped – did the girl sleep? There simply isn't the space to list all her inventions, achievements, firsts and adventures, she was extra-extraordinary.

Finally in 1955 the Fédération National d'Aéronautique at the Sorbonne presented her with possibly the medal she favoured most, for her exemplary work in medical aviation, despite her adversaries.

The quintessential adrenalin junkie and sportswoman extraordinaire, Marie continued to live life to the max. At the age of 80 she got her helicopter's pilot's licence and apparently flew in a US fighter jet that broke the sound barrier – why not, breaking barriers was her thing.

Mariya Oktyabrskaya
(1905–44)

Mariya Oktybrskaya was a Soviet hero, the eponymous tank girl who bulldozed her way through the Nazis after her beloved husband died in battle during the Second World War.

Mariya was born in 1905 in the Crimean Peninsula to a poor peasant family. She embraced the communist revolution in Russia and when she married, in 1925, she and her husband (whose name has proven most elusive) changed their surname to Oktybrskaya in honour of Russia's infamous October Revolution. Clearly she considered herself a comrade in arms with her husband. It was not out of the ordinary for Soviet women to learn the tricks of their husbands' trade if they were married to military men. Mariya was trained as a nurse but she also learned to shoot, handle weapons and drive vehicles and had joined the Military Wives Council.

When the Great Patriotic War (the Soviet name for the Eastern Front during the Second World War) began Mariya was evacuated to Tomsk in Siberia. Her husband who stayed to fight was struck down by the Nazi army in Kiev in 1941. However it took two years for Mariya to receive word of her husband's death, and she was understandably furious and devastated in equal measures.

She channelled her fury into the Soviet war effort and sold everything she had to purchase a T-34 tank for the war, costing 50,000 roubles. When she wrote to Stalin she offered her tank with the stipulation that she would drive it and it would be called *Boyevaya Podruga*. This has been interpreted to mean *Fighting Girlfriend* or *Frontline Female Comrade* tank.

Did Maria really go to war just as retribution for her husband's death, as is intimated in so many accounts? It seems a common theme to infer that women go to war to avenge their lovers' deaths as opposed to male reasons such as freedom and justice. By all accounts she was a staunch communist and she would have been vehemently against the Nazi incursions. Surely she joined the war for a multitude of reasons. Given this possible hypothesis, it seems female comrade was more suited to her personality.

The Soviet government allowed her to join the 26th Tank Battalion for propaganda purposes. Most believed she was a joke and fodder for a publicity stunt. That changed quickly after her first mission in Smolensk in 1943. She bombarded her way through enemy lines taking out gun nests and artillery guns. The tank was hit by gunfire; she disobeyed orders and leapt out to fix it amidst flying bullets. From then on the men in her unit called her mother. She repeatedly showed exemplary courage in further raids. When the tank's path was damaged, she jumped out and repaired its tracks whilst her crew covered fire from the turrets. Unfortunately it was during one such night raid in a village near Vitebsk when she leapt out to make repairs that she was hit in the head by shrapnel. She was taken to a military hospital near Kiev where she died. She was one of the few women to be awarded Russia's highest medal for valour but, like so many brave soldiers, it was awarded after her death.

Mary Anning
(1799–1847)

Mary Anning never went to school but is remembered as a brilliant palaeontologist – an expert in assessing and studying fossils to determine how and when they lived. She was born on 21 May 1799 to a very poor family in Lyme Regis, Dorset, the cliffs of which are rich in fossils from the Jurassic Period. The family couldn't afford to provide Mary with a formal education so she taught herself to read, write and draw.

Fossil bones were originally referred to as dragon's teeth and most people had little idea what they actually were, preferring instead to call them 'curiosities'. Regarded as the best in the fossil business, little is known or has been shared about Mary – probably because she was a woman doing what was perceived as a man's job, her family were poor and also because her astonishing finds, sold on to scientists, personal collections and museums, were rarely accurately attributed to her.

Mary's father was a carpenter and keen fossil hunter, who passed on his passion to her during their long fossil-hunting walks along the shore. She and her brother were the only surviving children of nine. Together they discovered the first complete ichthyosaur, Greek for 'fish lizard', in around 1810/1811, which has been displayed at London's Natural History Museum.

Mary was 10 when her father died in 1810, leaving them financially destitute. To make a living Mary sold fossils to visiting tourists, although the family was helped by several wealthy friends, including Lieutenant Colonel Thomas Birch, who sold his own fossil collection to provide for them. Mary would take over her father's fossil shop when she was 20.

The discovery of fossils would have literally blown the minds of scientists at the time – forcing them to completely re-assess their view on the natural world. Let's just say that Charles Darwin has a lot to thank Ms Anning for; her work led to the development of the Theory of Evolution. And many scientists wouldn't take Mary's work seriously until it was validated by (a man of course) anatomist Georges Cuvier, who confirmed its importance. She also discovered the first plesiosaurus (selling it for £100) which firmly established her reputation in the scientific world.

There's a great and very telling 1824 diary entry from Lady Harriet Sivester, who after meeting Mary wrote:

> The extraordinary thing in this young woman is that she has made herself so thoroughly acquainted with the science that the moment she finds any bones she knows to what tribe they belong. She fixes the bones on a frame with cement and then makes drawings and has them engraved . . . It is certainly a wonderful instance of divine favour – that this poor, ignorant girl should be so blessed, for by reading and application she has arrived to that degree of knowledge as to be in the habit of writing and talking with professors and other clever men on the subject, and they all acknowledge that she understands more of the science than anyone else in this kingdom.

In 1838 she would be awarded an annuity from the Geological Society of London and the British Association for the Advancement of Science.

Although the Geological Society didn't allow women members until 1904, they still recorded her death, of breast cancer, in 1847. The tongue-twister 'She sells seashells on the seashore', written around 1908, is thought to be about Mary and the fossilised coral Tricycloseris anningi is named in her honour.

Mary Edmonia Lewis
(*c.* 1844–1907 or 1843–1911)

Born in Greenbush, New York, Mary's Chippewa name was 'Wildfire' but she changed this as soon as she got to college.

Mary was the first professional African American sculptor. Her father was a free African-American and her mother a Chippewa Indian. Left as an orphan when she was young, she lived with her mother's tribe until she was 12.

Her studies at Oberlin College in Ohio from 1859, when she was only 15, had been funded by her brother Samuel Lewis, also known as 'Sunrise', who had left the Chippewa tribe to become a gold miner in California. The college was rare in that it admitted women and women of colour, but not everyone would welcome her. Mary wouldn't get to complete her art studies; on 27 January 1862, she was falsely accused of poisoning the spiced wine of her two white Oberlin roommates.

With uncertainty about her sexuality still prevalent today, there remains suspicion that, in an attempt to seduce them, Mary had spiked the women's drinks with an aphrodisiac. Although acquitted, she was beaten up by anti-abolitionists and left for dead. Her position at the college was untenable. She'd be a target for further abuse and harassment if she stayed.

Mary left for Boston to become a sculptor under the tutelage of Edward A. Brackett, who claimed prominent abolitionists amongst his clientele. Whilst there are very few surviving examples of her work, she was most famous for sculpting busts of famous abolitionists such as John Brown and Senator Charles Sumner; when seen through the prism of history and the fact that she was a black and famous artist at a time when slavery still persisted, her story and her art are all the more extraordinary.

Validated by her success, she travelled to Europe in 1865, settling in Rome, to work alongside an all-female group of sculptors. Her work was influenced by her Native American and African-American roots. She opened a showroom in Rome, was featured in prominent art magazines and was renowned for her work based on *The Song of Hiawatha*, the poem by Henry Wadsworth Longfellow, who would actually come to visit her in Italy.

Though there are very few surviving examples of her work, her most well-known sculpture was *The Death of Cleopatra*, now housed at the Smithsonian American Art Museum in Washington DC.

Mary returned to the US each year for various tours and in 1872 for an exhibition of her work at the San Francisco Art Association. Her date and place of death remain inconclusive, although a death certificate was discovered in London in 1907.

> There is nothing so beautiful as the free forest. To catch a fish when you are hungry, cut the boughs of a tree, make a fire to roast it, and eat it in the open air, is the greatest of all luxuries. I would not stay a week pent up in cities, if it were not for my passion for art.
>
> Mary Edmonia Lewis, quoted in 'Letter From L Maria Child', *National Anti-Slavery Standard*, 27 February 1864.

Mary Frith, aka Moll Cutpurse
(1584–1659)

In the seventeenth century men expected to control women in every aspect of society including the criminal underworld. It took a brave, stubborn lass to defy them. Enter Mary Frith, resplendent in her doublet (men's clothes), smoking a long, clay pipe, swearing like a trooper and dominating her criminal patch.

Despite Mary being born to a lowly shoemaker and housewife, she was taught to read in a brief window of time – during Queen Elizabeth Ist's reign – when girls were educated. She was a boisterous tomboy preferring to wield a sword rather than sewing needle. She scorned the gentle, pious life of 'good' women, revelling in fights, drinking and petty theft. Her contemporaries considered her an entertaining eccentric, whilst the puritanical authors of the eighteenth century were less enamoured.

She came to the public's attention in 1600 after being arrested for pickpocketing. Her uncle, a respectable minister, tried to reform her by shipping her off to New England. Mary had other ideas and fled from the ship, swimming back to shore and heading for London, where her career in crime took off.

She was the first 'ladette', carousing in the alehouses, drinking with the boys and would have set her farts on fire if she knew how. Her critics decried her as a shameless hussy, but mostly they were just buddies sharing a bawdy tale over a pint. Being such an exhibitionist, it was hardly a punishment when she was made to wear a white sheet at St Paul's Cross as penance for donning men's clothes. Society was scandalised and amused in equal measure, inspiring two plays about her called *The Madde Pranckes of Mery Mall of the Bankside* and *The Roaring Girl*.

During the Civil War she showed passionate support for the Cavaliers by becoming the original Dick Turpin, relieving Roundheads of their loot. Her highway spree ended when she was caught after robbing General Sir Thomas Fairfax. A handsome bribe saved her from the gallows. Instead she was sent to Bedlam, though hanging may have been preferable.

Once pronounced sane, she became a successful fence, managing her own money laundering empire. In pre-industrial Britain possessions were not mass-produced, and being unique stolen goods were difficult to sell. Fences effectively held these goods to ransom, giving thieves a cut of the money.

Mary did all this from her immaculate and feminine home on Fleet Street. She had three maids and several dogs, whom she pampered with home-cooked fare and their own bedrooms. Her home was filled with mirrors so she could gaze at herself as much as any selfie-taking narcissist today. There was more to her than met the eye.

Mary was a robust character. In her diary she gleefully relates teaching a barmaid a lesson for calling her Moll Cutpurse, a nickname she hated from her pickpocketing days. Mary bet the serving girl that her dog could tell if she was a virgin. She had trained her dog to only take meat from her right hand and Mary manipulated the maid to offer only from the left. The dog refused three times and so Mary declared that the maid had slept with three men, blackening her reputation.

Unfortunately in the end Mary, a woman filled with vitality and chutzpah, contracted dropsy disease which made her paranoid and delusional. She died in 1659.

Mary Seacole
(*c.* 1805–81)

Mary has only relatively recently come to historical prominence, portrayed as the mixed race version of the white Florence Nightingale. The real truth is more complicated and the two women's accomplishments are very different.

A commemorative bronze statue of Mary was unveiled outside St Thomas' Hospital in London in June 2016, inscribed with a quote from her war correspondent friend Sir William Howard Russell: 'I trust that England will not forget one who nursed her sick, who sought out her wounded to aid and succour them, and who performed the last offices for some of her illustrious dead.' It's the first public statue of a named black woman in Britain, although Mary herself would never have referred to herself as a black woman. She was proud of her Scottish and Creole heritage.

Fans of Florence Nightingale have taken great umbrage at the perceived slight; the hospital is where Ms Nightingale established a teaching school (the Florence Nightingale School of Nursing and Midwifery). They frostily point out that in stark comparison Mary never even worked in a hospital.

How about we don't compare them to each other at all and instead view them as two separate but equally headstrong, determined women who each made their own contributions to society. In the midst of the Victorian era, Mary was a mixed race woman who travelled, practised herbal medicine, ran various businesses and helped the war effort.

Mary Seacole was born Mary Jane Grant in Kingston, Jamaica to a Scottish soldier father and a free-born Jamaican mother (slavery existed in Jamaica until 1838) who practised traditional medicine, remedies and healing, as well as running a boarding house. There is no doubt that she passed on that knowledge to her daughter, who referred to herself and her mother as 'Doctress'.

Mary started her own small business on a journey to England, where she sold jams, pickles and other preserves. On her return to Jamaica, she married naval officer Edwin Horatio Seacole in 1836 and together they ran a shop.

After Edwin died in 1844 (her mother would die shortly afterwards), she spent time in Panama with her brother running her British Hotel for gold prospectors who were en route to California. She used some of her remedies to treat patients of the cholera epidemic, most notably and unfortunately using lead acetate and mercury.

As the Crimean War started, she travelled to London on business for her gold stocks. Whilst there, she applied to volunteer and join Florence Nightingale's nursing team but failed the interview. Was it because of racial prejudice? Or was it because she wasn't experienced enough or lacked a 'proper' education? Perhaps the truth is a combination of both.

Whatever the reasons, Mary wasn't going to let a word like 'no' stand in her way. Using money from her gold speculations and previous businesses, she self-funded her passage to the Crimea (actually meeting Florence Nightingale briefly en route in Scutari). She spent the first couple of weeks offering tea and lemonade to soldiers, before setting up the British Hotel with a family relative/business partner close to Balaclava in 1855. Calling it a hotel was a stretch; it had two rooms for boarders, a shop selling essential supplies such as blankets and boots and a refectory for army officers, offering hot food and drink. She set up her own mule train, transporting life-saving supplies, food and medicine to sell at the front lines across the war-torn region. She would also administer first aid to soldiers and cook food for them. They affectionately called her Mother Seacole.

At the end of the war in 1856 and on her return to London she was broke. In a show of unity and warm gratitude, the British army and newspapers worked together to raise money to help clear her debts and open a new store in Aldershot, although ultimately the new business failed. Financially supported by her British friends, she lived in comfort in Paddington, London until her death at the age of 76 in 1881.

Mary Shelley (30 August 1797– 1 February 1851) and the Ghosts of Fanny Imlay and Harriet Shelley

Fanny Imlay (1794–1816)

Mary Shelley is a gothic legend, her desperate tale of a monster and his far more monstrous creator has sent layers of fear through its readers, from a violent beast to our more deep-seated angst about existence and morality. And the book's own birth story takes place in just the type of dark and stormy night that all good ghost stories hail from. In 1816 Mary had run off with the romantic rebel Percy Shelley to Switzerland, where they joined Byron, the dark and brooding bad boy incarnate. In the company of these literary giants and against the backdrop of a stormy summer, Byron proposes a horror story competition, and *Frankenstein* is conceived, when she is just 19.

Her most famous novel, *Frankenstein* is just a pale reflection of the tragedy and horror that layer Mary's real world and that of the women who hung around these bohemian behemoths, Françoise (Fanny) Imlay and Harriet Shelley.

Fanny was Mary Shelley's half-sister. At just 22 she travelled alone to an unremarkable boarding house in Swansea. She went to her room and wrote a letter to explain that she no longer wanted to be a burden and that soon her existence would be forgotten. She then took a fatal dose of laudanum. Percy and Mary having received a disturbing letter raced to Wales but it was too little, too late.

What drove Fanny to such a lonely and tragic end? Fanny had the misfortune to live in the midst of the Romantic Movement's brightest and most self-absorbed stars. Whilst her mother Mary Wollstonecraft adored her daughter, describing her as vivacious and bright, her real father was a flaky American entrepreneur with no interest in her, and her step-father, William Godwin, dismissed her as mediocre. Her mother's immense personality as a celebrated feminist cast yet another shadow for Fanny to get lost in. In addition Godwin, who raised her, made it clear he believed Mary had inherited their mother's talent. Fanny was a great housekeeper, though.

And then in this bleak parody of a Grimm's fairytale, her mother died shortly after giving birth to her sister Mary. Fanny was only 5. When Godwin brought home Jane Clairmont, their step-mother, the girls couldn't stand her and Jane favoured her own children. Fanny was, perhaps, too self-conscious of her bastard status, a broken cuckoo in a shockingly bohemian nest. She passionately admired the brilliant minds that circled her – Percy was a frequent visitor and fan of Godwin's anarchic ideals, especially free love.

Living with this brilliance was another matter as their genius seemed entwined with deeply unpleasant narcissism. Godwin believed the world owed him a living but in the aftermath of the vicious Robespierre Terrors, the world had fallen out of love with his socialist radicalism. Like a begging Cinderella, it was left to Fanny to plead to patrons for more money. The increasing debt fell on her shoulders and the atmosphere in the household became progressively more hostile and bitter.

Mary and another sister Claire escaped by running off with Percy Shelley. Caught up in the daring, romantic whirlwind the teenage sisters left Fanny behind to deal with their father's fury and misery. There has been speculation that Fanny too had fallen for Percy's charms, adding a broken heart to the dismal situation.

Fanny could almost be a character from a bad penny dreadful, the woman in distress, abandoned with no protector living in a depressing atmosphere of tension at the mercy of self-serving and egotistical men.

Percy, the son of rich aristocracy and a huge admirer of Godwin, had been supporting him financially. But now Fanny had to ask him for more money whilst Godwin took the high ground and refused to talk to the disgraced teenagers. Where was his free-thinking, bohemian idealism now? When the Shelleys returned to England she found herself caught in the middle, and middlemen rarely fare well. By now Percy too was in debt and not inclined to fund Godwin. Fanny apparently begged to live with them when they were in Bath in 1818. They refused.

Finally after an unpleasant visit to Percy, Fanny boarded the train to Wales. Fearing the scandal for Godwin and himself, when Percy arrived in Swansea, he removed anything identifying her and destroyed her letters leaving her to be buried in an unnamed grave. They effectively erased a woman whose ordinariness had already rendered her negligible to the dramatic, genius world of the Godwins and Shelleys. Her tragedy inspired some of Percy's poetry – self-serving or genuinely devastated, we will never know as the family took such pains to cover up this shameful episode.

Harriet Shelley (1795–1816)

The dystopian fairy tale continues. Just a few weeks after Fanny's suicide Percy's first wife Harriet, aged 21, is found dead in the Serpentine Lake in Hyde Park. She is heavily pregnant and presumably killed herself, though conspiracies suggest Godwin murdered her so Percy could marry Mary. The evidence: his diary talks about Harriet's death before she is discovered – spooky.

Harriet also eloped with Percy at the age of 16 in what seems to be rather an unfortunate habit for the womanising poet. Again, they run off with another woman in tow, her sister. By this point the best spin doctor would have trouble rescuing Percy's reputation or so you would think.

Some rather vicious gossip suggested Harriet was pregnant by another man and therefore unworthy of pity, and Percy absolved himself of all responsibility by painting her as a hysterical depressive who emotionally blackmailed him into marriage by threatening suicide. Further tarnishing her image, he described her as an unnatural woman refusing to breastfeed their first baby – and let's all praise to god that we don't live in the nineteenth century anymore. It is several years before history rewrites Harriet's script more sympathetically.

Harriet had started married life as a giddy bride, eager to support and follow her husband everywhere. She is described by Percy's close friend Thomas Jefferson Hogg as always adapting to suit him as well as bright and intelligent. However after romancing her with poetry, Percy gets bored and moves in with another luscious beauty for some time. He always seems to come back to her, if only for short times, so it is very possible that she is pregnant with his baby when she is found in the lake.

After tiring of his current ladylove (free love after all or maybe just some murky values dressed up as high-minded ideals), Percy practically moves into the Godwin household. Depending on whether you are on Team Harriet or Team Mary, Mary seduces him or he seduces her by her mother's grave where she loves hanging out – each to their own. And then he elopes again leaving Harriet pregnant with their second child.

Never fear though because Mary and Percy generously invite Harriet along – as a sister or part of a *ménage à trois*? Luckily she has enough respect to tell them where to go and so they travel to Switzerland where Mary's other sister Claire Clairmont falls pregnant to Lord Byron who then ditches her – the last of the great Romantic poets?

When Percy's funds dry up, he asks Harriet for money to support him and Mary – it's getting harder and harder to work out why all those women fell for him, he must have had a large carrot to tempt them. By the time the newly-weds return to England Harriet, unsurprisingly, has suffered many spells of melancholy. By this point she is alone because her sister has taken Harriet's daughter to the country – another abandoned woman living in abject misery. She goes to live in Chelsea under the name of Harriet Smith, perhaps to save her family the scandal of her suicide.

Of course these women were not characters in a gothic piece of fiction, it was very real and none of them were all evil or all good. There should never be a Team Mary or Team Harriet. Harriet continues to appear in Percy's poetry and it is believed he was deeply affected by her death. All these people were so young – rebellious teenagers – influenced by the heady world of radical Enlightenment.

As for Mary Shelley herself, the years following her great escape with Percy and Claire were filled with tragedy and financial hardship. She was devastated by the loss of two children, they had returned to England to hide Claire's unmarried pregnancy, her father wouldn't talk to her and Percy continued his adulterous habits. It is likely Fanny's death hit her hard as the sisters, despite events, were close and Fanny had comforted her after the loss of her child.

One can only imagine how she processed so much loss. Her lack of reaction to Fanny's and Harriet's deaths may well have been a paralysing type of numbness or fear of scandal ruining her family who were already living precariously.

Alas there was no happy ending for Mary either as Percy himself drowned in a boating accident in 1822. Now a single mother, she managed to earn money writing to support her son – Percy's family wouldn't help and it is thanks to her continued promotion of Shelley's work that, for all his faults, we can read his amazing poetry. Her other novels such as *Mathilde*, though lesser known, are considered classics.

Mary Willcocks, aka Princess Caraboo (1791–1864)

Mary Willcocks was a Victorian journalist's dream. She sold newspapers as a mysterious 'oriental' princess and made even more headlines as the trickster who successfully hoodwinked the gullible upper classes.

The Victorians were fascinated by the 'Orient' and loved curling up to an exotic story of the lesser people who lived in a land far, far away. These idealised, inventive ideas were manna to Mary Willcocks when she burst into their lives one day as Princess Caraboo.

She was found wandering destitute in a small town near Bristol. Petite, pretty and wearing a black scarf,

turban-style, on her head, she spoke in a strange language and was taken to the county's magistrate Samuel Worral at his home in the awe-inspiring Knole Park. The benevolent Mrs Elizabeth Worral took her to a nearby inn but the next day the owner reported strange behaviour. She wouldn't sleep on the floor and performed some bizarre rituals. It was quite the mystery and captivated Elizabeth Knowles, who brought her home.

News of this exotic creature spread and many gentlemen and 'experts' came to investigate. She delighted them with strange practices: fasting on a Tuesday; only eating certain food; praying over cups of tea (no matter how deeply an English person may involve themselves in a fraud, they will never pass up a cup of tea); and, their favourite, swimming naked.

When Portuguese traveller Manuel Eynesso visited and proclaimed he could understand her language, he inadvertently provided her with a plausible and brilliant back story. He told the delighted gentry that this beautiful heroine was in fact a royal princess from the island of Javasu. She had been captured by pirates but daringly managed to escape and swim to nearby English shores.

It was a fantastic concoction of a glamourous, tropical stranger blended with the snobbery of blue blood – a story Victorian society lapped up. Mary was staggeringly consistent, never uttering a word of English even when startled.

Alas the truth was far more prosaic and her fame would be her undoing. Mrs Neale, a landlady from Bristol, recognised Mary as an old lodger from one of her many portraits in the newspapers. It transpired that Mary came from the not so very far away land of Dorset, the daughter of a humble cobbler and had a truly chequered employment record. Previous employers, of which there were many, said she behaved very strangely and would often run away. In fact 'Princess Caraboo' was not the first of the many fantastical creations and strange situations that she invented for herself. (There was also an intrepid tale of being kidnapped by highwaymen.) Mary either suffered from poor mental health and may even have believed her fantasies or she was a cunningly clever con artist.

Consciously or not she brilliantly bought into the fervour surrounding orientalism and the eagerness of people to prove their knowledge and experience. People were desperate for Princess Caraboo to be real. Fortunately, after she fessed up, she wasn't thrown to the wolves. The poorer members of society applauded her for ridiculing the high and mighty. Elizabeth sent her to Philadelphia in 1817 where her notoriety had spread and she gave performances as Princess Caraboo. She returned to England in 1824, performing until interest waned. In the end she married and got a job delivering leeches to hospitals. For all her earlier fame, rather sadly she ended up buried in an unmarked grave.

Mary Wollstonecraft
(27 April 1759–10 September 1797)

Mary was in a league of her own. Her achievements would be impressive for the modern woman of today; for a woman of the eighteenth century, they defied convention and were simply extraordinary.

A true intellectual, feminist, advocate for women's education, philosopher, traveller, historian – her story is endlessly fascinating. She also tried every avenue available to a woman of the time (lady's companion, governess, teacher) before finding her true calling as a writer and champion of the Enlightenment.

Born in London's Spitalfields, the second child of seven, her life's experiences would leave her with bouts of depression and shape her feminist outlook and views on marriage. She was the daughter of a drunk, abusive father and a mother who welcomed her death as a release from the restrictions of her life, and sister to an older brother Ned who would in contrast to his sisters enjoy an incredible education. Mary was a woman light years ahead of her time. She railed against life's injustices against women and their place in society.

In 1784 she would set up a girls school with her sisters Eliza and Everina and close friend Fanny Blood. She would also help Eliza escape a suspected abusive marriage. She attempted life as a governess to the children of Irish nobles Lord and Lady Kingsborough, but she soon realised that a) she despised Lady Kingsborough and b) being a governess was not for her. Although in a bizarre twist of fate, in later years, Kingsborough's daughter Margaret King would form a strong friendship with Mary's own daughter Mary Shelley.

The experience inspired 'Thoughts on the Education of Daughters', a pamphlet published in 1787, after which she became a full-time writer. She learned French, Italian and German, contributed a considerable number of articles to the *Analytical Review* and translated many important works of European literature and philosophy.

At the heart of a vibrant literary, artistic and intellectual salon, she made her name by writing the 'Vindication of the Rights of Men' in 1790, a letter in response to a colleague's book on the French Revolution; the first edition was published anonymously, only the second edition bearing her own name.

A 'Vindication of the Rights of Woman', two years later, was earth-shattering for its time. Translated into multiple languages, it confronted the leaders of the French Revolution head on, called for a revolution by women to enable them to have equal rights, independence and sovereignty over their own lives. Mary travelled to Revolutionary France, lived through the Terror and witnessed Louis XVI lose his head to Madame La Guillotine – an experience that haunted her.

Abandoned by her feckless American lover Gilbert Imlay, with whom she would have her first daughter, Fanny Imlay, she attempted suicide twice (the first with laudanum, the second time in the River Thames).

As for her famed love affair with political writer William Godwin, it was mutual dislike at first sight when they met in 1791 but better luck second time around. They lived together for a while but when Mary became pregnant decided, rather conversely for a feminist, that the scandal of being an unwed mother would be too much to bear. They married with little fuss on 29 March 1797 and created a living arrangement that Helena Bonham Carter and Tim Burton were probably inspired by. Godwin rented his own separate rooms to work in during the day and would return to their shared home in Somers Town in the evenings.

Mary went into labour on 30 August and in a tragically stupid set of circumstances when the placenta didn't come out naturally, the attending doctor decided to rip it out himself. Infection soon set in and she died on 10 September 1797 at the age of 38. The heartbroken Godwin was too distraught to attend the funeral. Their daughter was Mary Shelley (1797–1851), author of *Frankenstein*. Her life was in many ways to mirror that of her mother.

She left unfinished 'Maria, or the Wrongs of Woman' (an unofficial follow-up to 'Vindication of the Rights of Woman') which marked a new direction in her feminist thinking. Writing through the voice of a prostitute, it expressed a desire for political and legal reform to better the lot of all women, regardless of their place or ranking in society. Because of her unorthodox lifestyle (pregnant twice whilst unmarried) it took a while for her legacy as a feminist, writer and philosopher to be properly recognised. She was a role model for the suffragettes and remains so today for the modern woman who navigates her own complicated path.

Mata Hari, or Margaretha Zelle (7 August 1876–15 October 1917)

The name Mata Hari seems to evoke associations of wanton sexual promiscuity used as a tool of betrayal. However in the same way that the name Mata Hari is made up, the associations also have a strong element of fiction to them. Most recently a new collection of letters written by the infamous Mata Hari herself cast new doubts on the image of her as a scheming seductress traitor.

The problem in detangling her story is the degree to which she invented numerous personas and stories herself. Combine this with a trial that based itself on circumstantial evidence as well as a large degree of embellishment, and her life emerges as an orchestrated piece of fiction. Sadly this fiction never had a happy ending and led her to a firing squad.

Born in Holland to a wealthy family, her father's investments went belly up and he was forced to declare bankruptcy. Having being spoiled and cosseted by an adoring father, Margaretha (her actual name) suddenly found herself bereft as he left the family to try and restore his fortunes. The strain was too much and her parents divorced whilst he shacked up with another woman in Amsterdam. To compound her misery, when her mother died, she and her brothers were split up and sent to various relatives across the country.

Perhaps it's not a great surprise that at just 17 she answered an ad for a wife from a Dutch officer twenty years her senior. Unfortunately the marriage was not the great romantic escape from dreary Holland that she hoped and nor was it a dream for her husband Rudolph Macleod. Both were bitterly unhappy in a relationship punctuated by vicious arguments, infidelity and tragedy. She also alleged that Rudolph was physically abusive and he was certainly a confirmed alcoholic.

A particularly tragic and mysterious episode was the death of their 2-year-old son Norman who, along with his sister Nonnie, became violently ill from either food poisoning or, as some alleged, the nanny did it. Margaretha suggested the nanny was bitter following a liaison with Rudolph. Their marriage disintegrated shortly after. When he refused to pay her enough money to survive, she was forced to leave her daughter Nonnie with him whilst she tried to seek work.

And it was from this period after 1904, when Margaretha left her husband and before she emerged as Mata Hari in Paris, that the newly discovered letters are from. They show a woman devastated at leaving her daughter behind and desperately searching for work as a lady's companion or riding horses in a circus, she tries everything until she concludes that her sexual allure is the best way for her to survive financially.

And she begins to invent a new persona. Having been maligned in Indonesia whilst married for being a half-caste thanks to her dark colouring, she turns it into an advantage. Riding on the wave of orientalism that is sweeping Parisians off their feet, she becomes an exotic oriental dancer called Mata Hari, sometimes the daughter of an eastern prince and sometimes a priestess. There's no Google to betray her boring Dutch roots and Paris laps it up. She is the spicy toast of society, dressing erotically and often nude in theatres and private salons and performing Burlesque-style dances wearing sheer materials and shedding layers throughout her routine. Exotic music and scenery added to the atmosphere. She became famous for being a courtesan as well as for her sensual dances, travelling throughout Europe and living very well.

However, the outbreak of the First World War spelt the end of the good times. Mata Hari was in Germany when the news broke, and being considered French, they confiscated her assets leaving her to return to Amsterdam broke. Added to this the theatres were shutting down and the nation's mood changed to a more serious tone no longer interested in the frivolous life she represented.

Her story becomes complex to unravel from this point. She claims she was asked to spy by the Germans who knew she had liaisons with important men and that she threw the invisible ink they gave her into the canal. She then says she agreed to become a double agent for France. When the Allies put her on trial it seemed a travesty of circumstantial evidence, missing witnesses, mistaken identities and possibly contrived documents. Did the French stitch her up to show they were capturing dangerous dissidents whilst the war bled the country dry on the battlefields; or was Germany playing a bluff by misdirecting the French to Mata Hari with false documents to divert their attention; or was Mata Hari trying to play off two countries in a naive and stupid way? Spies in novels may always be based on the Mata Hari idea of a beautiful temptress, anyone seen James Bond, but in reality the best spy fades into the crowd and is unremarkable. If Mata Hari was anything she was far from unremarkable.

When she was sentenced to execution she was in denial, her years in the jail were marked by desperation and despair but when she walked out to face the firing squad she blew kisses at the soldiers and refused a blindfold. She looked them straight in the eye as they shot her dead.

Maw Broon
(Created 1936)

Many Scots would agree that their own creation Maw Broon from the Dudley Watkins comic strips deserves a place in this pantheon of women. She was the matriarch of the Broon family of Auchenstoggle and a metaphorical mother to many. All the fans feel a sense of reassurance and comfort when they cuddle up to this 'braw' family, especially devoted to the Scots dialect that permeates every story.

She may be fictional but she was also a representative, a blueprint of the ideal mother and woman especially in the 1930s when the comics began. Scotland's *Sunday Post* and the cartoons creator's have been accused of right-wing romanticism and feminists would have a thing or two to say about the character of Maw but there's no escaping the historical context and the continuing love for these down-to-earth characters despite all this.

The Broons were a light-hearted picture of working class Scots in the pre-war period. They provided safe stories with many a slapstick and Aesopian moral woven into them to distract from the depression of the 1930s. Like so many cartoons, the Broons never age and their family life seems stuck in a halcyon past with a few modern gadgets thrown in over the years. They take Scotland through the war and all the decades that follow, only ever intending to be a cheery wee escape from real life.

She would never be chosen as a poster child for feminism. Her character was intended to embody quite parochial, right-wing values of the self-sacrificing matriarch who gets fair worn 'oot' from the housework, the cooking and her family acting like daft 'galoots' (idiots). She would be black-affronted (ashamed) by their antics. However she ends up being the voice of reason in most of the stories.

Most often it was the men's' pride in being machismo and their hare-brained schemes that inevitably led to humorous misunderstandings or crazy outcomes. In one tale the brothers and their father are showing off their muscles, each trying to outdo the other in the number of weights they can lift. In comes Maw exclaiming about the mess and she promptly lifts the entire box of weights and tidies them away.

Maw stood out as the calm and moral member of the family. Built like the robust figureheads on ships, she was indeed the stalwart captain who steered her wayward yet intrinsically good family.

She is a reassuring presence embedded in the culture of Scotland.

Maxine Elliot
(5 February 1873–5 March 1940)

The captivating, world-famous actress Maxine Elliot was born Jessie Carolyn Dermott in Rockland, Maine in the US. Her father was an Irish-born naval captain. Her mother Adelaide Hill would suffer bouts of melancholy and depression before being committed to and eventually dying in a mental institution.

Pregnant at 14 by a local rake, Arthur Hall, she conveniently departed on a five-month trip to South America with her Irish father. The baby either died or she miscarried. On her return she was sent to boarding school. After visiting New York, she would marry a wealthy, flash 30-year-old lawyer, George A. McDermott. She was 16. It wasn't a great marriage. He was an alcoholic gambler who would beat her and she returned home divorced and despondent, before leaving again at the age of 21 for New York to take to the stage, despite the disapproval of her father.

She would change her name to Maxine Elliot in 1889. Despite her lack of acting experience, she worked hard as part of a touring theatre group and climbed the acting ladder. She would marry comedian Nat C. Goodwin in 1898, who presented her with her own railroad car as a wedding gift. They would tour the country and star together in various plays to packed audiences and to public acclaim. They were hugely popular and successful celebrities. She mixed in high-society circles and on one visit to London was presented to King Edward VII. She and Goodwin would divorce in 1908, after which there are unsubstantiated rumours that she had an affair with the septuagenarian banker J.P. Morgan.

Having the acquaintance of J.P. Morgan didn't hurt her financial prospects either. Together with Broadway impresarios the Shubert brothers, he put up half the money when in 1908 she bought and named her own 725-seat theatre, the Maxine Elliot Theatre on New York's Broadway. She would be the only woman in the US to both own and manage her own theatre company. A savvy business woman, she negotiated profitable acting contracts for herself and made a fortune as an investor and stock trader with properties in both the US and England, one of them in Bushey Heath, Hertfordshire.

In 1913 she began an affair with New Zealand tennis player Tony Wilding, fifteen years her junior. They were due to marry and she was utterly devastated by his death in the First World War at the age of 31. He was serving with the Royal Marines.

During the First World War she would channel her considerable talent, charms and fortune into humanitarian work. She enlisted with the Red Cross as a nurse and used much of her own money to finance rescue efforts for Belgian citizens trapped by the German invasion. She bought a huge barge (300 tonnes) and from February 1915 to May 1916 it travelled through the canals of Belgium providing essential medical, food and relief supplies to the starving and desperate populace. Belgium would award her the Order of the Crown for her philanthropic efforts.

She bought a stunning villa on the French Riviera, which welcomed guests including Winston Churchill and the Duke of Windsor. Prince Aly Khan would purchase it at the end of the war. She would return to acting in 1917 only to retire from the stage in 1920, determined as ever to do things her way and step down at the height of her powers.

She died in Cannes, the south of France, from a heart attack on 5 March 1940.

Messalina
(AD 17–48)

You can't help but relish in the utter depravity of the infamous Roman nymphomaniac Messalina, aka Emperor Claudius's wife, as told in salacious tales from ancient Roman scholars to the more contemporary and hugely popular *I Claudius* by Robert Graves. However her true story is lost amidst political bias and the lurid minds of some very dirty old men.

It seems Roman men couldn't decide the best way to destroy a woman's name. One minute they were trying to erase Messalina from history by banishing and removing every trace of her. Then several years later Roman historians had resurrected her in their accounts as one of the most depraved and sexually deviant women to have graced Caesar's palace. By making her so scandalous they assured her place in history, art and literature.

These historians included famous scholars such as Pliny the Elder, Tacitus and the poet Juvenal. They were likely motivated by a hatred for the Imperial royal bloodline, and a yearning for the glorious Republic. You'd be forgiven for thinking these stories belonged in a sex pamphlet, the type found in a sperm donor's cubicle. Pliny wrote an exciting romp about the night Messalina challenged a prostitute to see who could sleep with the most men in a night. Apparently it was twenty-five – game set and match to Lady M.

Juvenal named her the 'Whore Princess'. His famous satires describe how she snuck out of the palace in disguise and hurried to a brothel. Here she had her own 'red-light' chamber where she could have sex until dawn and then 'reluctantly' sneak back to Claudius's bed.

Messalina was also painted as a scheming, power-mad traitor who held the 'weak and feeble' Claudius by the balls. The historian Tacitus was particularly eloquent, claiming she convinced Claudius of numerous plots against him, resulting in a series of exiles, executions and suicides.

Depicting Claudius as the beleaguered cuckold, a hen-pecked emperor would have been a clever nail in the Imperial Caesar government. Presenting Messalina as a rampantly sexual manipulator suited republican historians's agendas.

The proverbial last straw was when she married another man whilst Claudius was away. Did she do this for sexual reasons or, more likely, as a last-ditch attempt to secure power for her son Britannicus. Before she had a chance to persuade Claudius that 'it's not what it looks like', his servants had killed her, believing this to be a political deposition.

But what was the truth? Did she really have the libido of a randy teenage boy overdosing on Viagra? Did she cheerfully and ruthlessly eradicate every opponent to her son's succession? We will never know her own thoughts let alone those of her supporters thanks to the sanctions imposed against her name after her treasonous *coup d'état*.

It's likely any misdeeds keeping her awake at night arose from a guilty conscience about political opponents she viciously put down rather than from a night at the whorehouse. Few characters from Roman history fare well in those terms, and many of them dealt with their enemies the same way.

Mileva Maric
(19 December 1875–4 August 1948)

It could often be said that behind every truly great male theoretical physicist is usually his wife, an arguably equally brilliant physicist, who didn't get the recognition she deserved because her husband was not a very nice man. We're talking about Mileva Maric, who until relatively (pun intended) recently was known only as Albert Einstein's first wife.

Born in Serbia in 1875, her liberal-minded father arranged for her not only to attend the male-only Royal Classical High School in Zagreb, but later to attend physics lectures which were otherwise closed to girls. She was top of the class for maths and physics.

In 1896 Albert and Mileva met as students at the Polytechnic Institute in Zurich and shared a passion for physics and for each other. She was the only woman in her group of students. As their studies progressed they would often be similarly matched in grades, although Mileva would fall at the final hurdle in her last teaching diploma exams. Three months pregnant with Albert's daughter Liserl, she attempted the exam once more only to fail again. The baby, born in January 1902, then disappears from public view. No records of her survive – it is not known what happened to her.

Despite the objections of his family, Albert and Mileva would marry on 6 January 1903 and live together for ten years. However they often spent long periods apart, when she would suffer from bouts of depression. Their sons Hans-Albert and Eduard followed on 14 May 1904 and 28 July 1910 respectively.

Their mutual passion for intellectual stimulus, ideas and learning would continue. They would study side by side, Albert making it clear in his correspondence that his brilliant wife's influence was indispensable to him, although as his star began to shine she would increasingly take on all the traditional domestic duties of a 'good' wife, and he would find other scientists to play with.

Whilst they had done the work and study together, any published material was under his name only; perhaps they feared their studies wouldn't be taken seriously if a woman's name was attached to them? Or perhaps naively Mileva thought their relationship, work and personal, would stand the test of time and co-authorship of their work was just a detail. They were both open about the team effort of their scientific studies in their correspondence. Mileva however would never have any theories or papers written solely in her name.

That is until it all began to unravel. In 1912 Albert had an affair with his cousin Elsa Lowenthal; Mileva would take the boys and move to Zurich. Einstein sent her an astonishing list of demands that he insisted must be met if they were to stay together, including that his laundry was done, she'd provide him with three meals a day, he refused to go out or travel with her and that under no circumstances was she to expect conjugal relations. What a prince of a man.

They would live apart until their eventual divorce in 1919. Upon their eventual split, she insisted that any money he might receive from winning the Nobel Prize for his 1905 paper on special relativity go to her, which it did in the divorce settlement. This could arguably be proof that she at the very least contributed to his work, if only, as critics of this idea suggest, as a sounding board. Albert would go on to marry Elsa just three months after the divorce was made final, although he didn't stay faithful to her either.

Any attempts after that by Mileva's family and friends to fight for equal-name recognition on Einstein's work were met with a strong wall of resistance from him, his legal team and those hell-bent on preserving his reputation. In letters Albert would even mock her, saying that if it weren't for his accomplishments no one would even pay attention to her.

Mileva would die alone at the age of 72 in Zurich.

Mirabal Sisters

Patria Mercedes Mirabal (1924–25 November 1960)
Minerva Argentina Mirabal (1926–25 November 1960)
Antonia Maria Teresa Mirabal (1935–25 November 1960)

The tremendous bravery shown by the Mirabal sisters of the Dominican Republic warrants proper use of the phrase awe-inspiring in a way that should strike awesome from the Californian lexicon forever. Such courageous martyrs come along rarely, male or female.

And who would have guessed that these well-to-do, middle-class, Catholic-educated mums would become such defiant revolutionaries that rallied a nation. Patria, Minerva and Maria Teresa are remembered reverently as Les Mariposas – the butterflies, after their secret codename. Like their namesake, these beautiful and vital sisters would forfeit their lives too soon.

They lived under the tyrannical rule of Trujillo, who was almost a caricature of an evil dictator so closely did his regime follow every rule in the Dummies Guide to being a Dictator – spies check, disappearances check, unexplained deaths of those who spoke out check, infamous torture prisons check, complete control of the country's infrastructure check, gags on media check, check and check. He ruled by fear instilling terror in all his subjects. No one knew when someone might inform on them for criticising Trujillo's government, his ears were everywhere and then it was a one-way ticket to hell. However Trujillo used his bully boy tactics on the wrong woman and his treatment of Minerva and her sisters would be the proverbial last straw for the Dominican people.

The trouble began for the sisters in 1949 after Trujillo invited the Mirabal family to one of his infamous parties – he had a penchant for young girls and he had his eye on Minerva. To refuse to go was tantamount to lunacy. However when he apparently tried it on, Minerva slapped him down resoundingly (some would say she actually slapped him) and the family left the party. Other accounts claim they left the party because they got caught outside in bad weather. Either way, the dictator was famous for being incredibly touchy to any perceived slight and leaving without his permission was not on. He was out for their blood now.

Their father was arrested and treated savagely – he would be arrested several times and the strain wrecked his health resulting in his early death in 1953. The family finances were ruined, Minerva's promising law career sabotaged before it even began and they became pariahs as people feared the repercussions of associating with them. In that same year of 1949 Minerva and her mother were put under house arrest at a hotel when they visited the capital. Some sources believe she was given the ultimatum to sleep with Trujillo or stay there but she escaped.

However far from breaking them his treatment ignited their spark of resistance into fully-fledged rebellion. The sisters had all married husbands that were also fervently anti-Trujillo. Together in 1959 they launched the organisation the Movement of the Fourteenth of June, named after a failed coup. It was led by Minerva and her husband.

Devastatingly the group was betrayed and hundreds were hauled to prison. However Trujillo once again underestimated his people – this time the wrath of the Catholic Church at the imprisonment of women and he felt compelled to release them. He kept the sisters's husbands in jail though in the hope it would curb their dogged rebellion. Ha – what did I just say about underestimating?

As he became more insecure and paranoid about being overthrown, he blamed the sisters more and more. In 1960 Minerva and Maria were arrested twice and sent to the infamous torture prison La Caruenta. This was not enough and he ordered their assassination in a singularly botched cover-up. All three sisters were intercepted on the way to visit their husbands, who had purposely been located in a remote prison.

Their jeep was ambushed and they were dragged into nearby fields. Trujillo's henchmen beat them mercilessly and then strangled them to death. They were then put back in the jeep and sent over a cliff to make it look like an accident. A murder – with the girls' clearly battered bodies and fingerprints everywhere – which Miss Marple could have solved in her sleep. Gross barbarity and gross stupidity.

It was too much. The Dominican citizens were horrified and resistance notched up several gears. Trujillo was assassinated six months later. As the people fought for freedom the legacy of the sisters encouraged many women to join the fight, although it would be a long time before democracy was restored.

Now the sisters are remembered every 25 November on the UN-designated International Day for the Elimination of Violence Against Women, dedicated in honour of their sacrifice, courage and devastating story.

Moremi Ajaso
(Twelfth Century)

In recalling the bravery of a tribal queen and violent encounters between warring factions the legend of the spy Queen of the Yoruba has a strong element of cultural and historical truth about it.

Originally from Offa, she was married to Oranmiyan, the King of Ile-Ife in south-west Nigeria, whose people were being targeted and continuously attacked and kidnapped for the slave trade by a neighbouring forest tribe, the Igbo. Moremi vowed to do everything she could to put a stop to them. Despite her husband's protestations, she determined to go undercover and made a deal with the river goddess Esimirin, who guaranteed success if Moremi would offer a great sacrifice.

The deal being struck, she allowed herself to be kidnapped and was taken before her enemy's king. He was immediately besotted with her, made her a wife and took her into his confidence. Before long she discovered that the tribespeople who so terrified her own dressed up in camouflage-like raffia from the forest and wore face masks. Needless to say, to the unsuspecting Yoruba they looked like otherworldly monsters and scared the beetle-juice out of them. The Igbo king, who clearly hadn't read the twelfth-century best-selling military mantra 'What Not To Tell the Beautiful Spy Pretending To Be A Prisoner of War', confided that the raffia, made of dry-grass, was extremely flammable.

Moremi escaped back to the Yoruba and breathlessly revealed the weakness to her husband. Delighted with her bravery, intelligence and initiative, he reinstated her as princess consort and started preparations for a fightback. Sure enough, at the next raid, the Yoruba used fire-arrows to fight against their enemies, who duly went down in a blaze of glory. The river goddess then claimed her end of the bargain; Moremi naively thought a buffet of cows and bullocks would suffice. Unfortunately, the river goddess insisted that Moremi sacrifice her own son Ela, which she did, leaving her bereft.

In recognition of the staggeringly high price she had paid for their freedom, the tribespeople vowed to hold an annual festival in her honour in the hope that Ela would return. As part of that tradition, in 2016 the current and fifty-first Ooni (ruler) of Ile-Ife Prince Adeyeye Enitan Ogunwusi unveiled a statue, the tallest in Nigeria, of Moremi to commemorate her courage. There is also a Moremi Beauty Pageant, part of a concerted effort to harness the Moremi legend to create a female ambassador for Yoruba, promoting culture, tourism and female empowerment.

Nanny and the Maroons
(1686–1733)

Jamaica's Koromantees were such fearsome leaders of the Maroon rebellions that they nearly brought the British to their knocking knees. They came from the Gold Coast in Ghana, mainly from the Ashanti and Akan tribes. And in those tribes women knew their place – as revered and respected leaders in spiritual, agricultural and, for some, military spheres. They weren't going to take any nonsense. It's no surprise that the awe-inspiring guerrilla and spiritual leader Nanny Maroon hailed from these proud people.

Nanny was the leader of the Windward Maroons and took control of the mountainous Nanny Town in 1720. Her story is wrapped up in legend, oral storytelling and jaundiced 'historical' reporting from the British colonials whose backsides she so skillfully whipped. Separating 'Legend' Nanny from 'flesh and bones' Nanny is not important because her symbolic representation of a strong and free mama gave slaves their strength to escape, and future generations the pride they needed when recovering from slavery. She is Mother Jamaica. Some historians believe there may even have been more than one nanny – that means a whole slew of hard-core rebel women. No wonder the British sent letters home pleading for help.

The practice of obeah (similar to Haiti's voodoo) was a crucial element of Maroon resistance and culture. Nanny was a shaman in obeah and her rituals were considered crucial to the success of the rebellions. The legends recount tales of Nanny bouncing bullets off her body, and some versions claim she even sucked the bullets in and then farted them out at the enemy. That's a potent magic in more ways than one.

Maroon successes encouraged plantation slaves to escape knowing there was a community to join. Maroons often raided plantations taking food, ammunition and slaves to swell their numbers – especially female slaves as family life was difficult in the harsh conditions they existed in. Historians agree, however grudgingly, that women were vital to Maroon survival. Their agricultural expertise kept starvation at bay. Women were also credited with charging plantations wielding large knives and terrifying their enemy.

Nanny wasn't just brawn, she was brains too. She was considered a master in strategy, guerrilla warfare and camouflage. She would dress her soldiers so expertly as trees that even a dog looking for a place to cock its leg might be fooled.

Nanny Town was situated in mountains which could only be accessed by a single-file footpath, meaning British soldiers could be picked off one by one, allowing a tiny number of Maroons to hold their ground. Captain Stoddart finally captured the town using cannon in 1734. The stories diverge here. Some believe Nanny and several of her people died. Others claim the community had already evacuated and Stoddart was left with nowt but some abandoned huts. When a treaty was signed in 1739 to end the wars, it was said that Nanny was unhappy that the treaty stipulated Maroons must support the British and return escaping slaves. This was unacceptable because it wasn't just physical freedom at stake, it was also ideological survival. Therefore one legend claims she carried on fighting, backed by loyal supporters, but she was forced to battle the black men who'd agreed to help the British suppress the rebellions. In the end she was shot dead because her obeah could not protect her from bullets fired by black men. However many historians believe that Nanny was dead long before the Windward Maroons signed the treaty.

Her name invokes pride in her descendants, recalling their history of one of the few successful African rebellions – and under the guidance of a woman no less.

Neerja Bhanot
(1963–86)

The stereotype of the air stewardess is as pervading and derogatory as those held to ridicule in a million blonde jokes. Yet these are the people who are in the front line when disaster strikes on board. Airplanes may be safer than riding in a car until a problem occurs, then it tends to be pretty damn terrifying.

We all wonder how we would react if placed in mortal danger. Luckily for the crew and passengers of Pan Am Flight 73 on 5 September 1986, Neerja Bhanot, the chief purser (stewardess in charge of the crew), showed amazing presence of mind and valiantly sacrificed her life when four terrorists hijacked the flight.

Neerja Bhanot had already shown herself to be a courageous and independent young woman after leaving an abusive marriage in the 1980s. She was born in 1962 to a loving family in Chandigarh, Punjab, India. A much longed for daughter, she was affectionately known by her family as Lado, meaning loved one.

Neerja was scouted by a photographer when she was a schoolgirl to appear as the 'girl next door' in a modelling shoot. She went on to become a successful model appearing in many adverts across India. To please her family, she agreed to an arranged marriage in 1985 and flew to the Gulf to live with her new husband. While there, she was subjected to hostile demands for a dowry, no access to money, verbal abuse and starved. When she returned to India for a modelling shoot, her husband sent a letter with a series of demands including cutting off contact with her family. Neerja decided to leave him, a bold move for a traditional girl, but she had the support of her family.

Soon after that decision she applied for the role of air steward with Pan Am and she was one of a small number selected from 10,000 applicants. Such a job was considered very prestigious and she was delighted to join the company. Her training may have covered service duties but security drills were and still are a priority.

So when Flight 73 landed for a stopover in Pakistan's Jinnah International Airport in the early morning en route to Frankfurt, all the staff had been trained to deal with terrorist activity. Four armed Palestinian hijackers from the Aby Nidal Organisation boarded the plane in the guise of airport security. Led by Zayd Safarini, their mission was to fly to Cyprus and Israel and demand the release of Palestinian prisoners before blowing up the plane.

Neerja quickly realised what was happening and immediately sent a secret hijack code to the pilots enabling them to escape through a secret hatch and therefore ground the plane – an approved plan in such a situation. As chief purser she was now first in command of a critical hostage situation, and one that got increasingly worse when the hijackers realised they needed a new cabin crew. When they shot dead American Indian Rajesh Kumar, aged 29, before throwing him onto the tarmac, there was no doubting the danger for all aboard. They demanded the crew collect everyone's passports, presumably to look for American passengers who were the primary targets. Neerja ensured that any American passports were hidden or thrown secretly down a rubbish chute as she and her crew collected passports.

The plane was then held for 17 hours as tensions ratcheted out of control. When the flight's auxiliary power ran out at 9.55 am, the plane was plunged into darkness igniting the pressure cooker on board. One hijacker shot at the explosive belt of his comrade, only just missing but triggering the men to start shooting indiscriminately. Neerja and a passenger threw themselves at the emergency doors managing to open them so passengers could jump outside. It was reported that Neerja could easily have leapt from the plane at this point but she stayed to help everyone off. As she shielded three children while they got on the chute to slide to safety she was gunned down by the terrorists. She later died of her injuries. One of those children would later become the captain of another airline and owed his life to Neerja.

She was posthumously awarded the Ashoka Chakra, India's highest award for valour. The terrorist leader was sent to an FBI prison and questions remain about what happened to the other men. Her parents set up the Neerja Bhanot Pan Am Trust to assist women overcoming social injustice and flight personnel who act beyond the call of duty – those heroic yet disparagingly labelled 'waitresses of the skies'.

Nur Jahan or Mehr-un-Nisa
(1577–1645)

Nur Jahan – a romantic tale of a loving couple who ruled together wisely? Or was she a scheming opportunist who manipulated her husband to sow discord and rule as she saw fit?

What is agreed is that she was the most influential and powerful woman in the Mughal Dynasty. She was born when her family had fallen on hard times and was en route to India. However her father Mirza Ghias Beg heralded her birth as a sign that their fortunes were changing. Although known as Nur Jahan, he named her Mehr-un-Nisa which means 'Sun Amongst Women' and prophetically she would light up their path. Soon after he was appointed to a great job at the Mughal court. As Nur gained power so too did her family. Her brother Asaf Khan was appointed prime minister under her rule.

And all of Nur's accomplishments were achieved behind the curtain of purdah – the seclusion of women from men and strangers. Whatever one thinks of purdah Mughal girls were well educated in both academia and martial skills. After Nur's first husband died she came to live in the emperor's harem as a lady-in-waiting to the begum (the wife of highest rank). Men in raincoats may fantasise about a paradise of lascivious lovelies but in reality a harem was a complex community. It included all the women in the emperor's family, their ladies-in-waiting, slaves, cooks, entertainers, guards and eunuchs – the only men permitted in the harem aside from the emperor himself.

In the spring of 1611 Nur caught the Emperor Jahinger's eye at the Meena Bazzar and they were married soon after. This was remarkable because Nur was a widow in her 30s, which set her firmly on the shelf. She was considered exceptionally beautiful just like all good princesses and she became Jahinger's favourite wife; number 20. But she did more than look pretty. She was an expert marksman and is famous for taking down a tiger with one shot, despite the obscured vision afforded by the howdah, a canopied seat atop an elephant. Unsurprisingly, when the emperor's begum died she was immediately honoured with that rank.

Nur may have been a crack shot but her husband was a crack addict. By 1622 Jahinger's battle with booze and drugs was well documented and Nur had been given unprecedented powers for a woman to approve all orders in his name. She also improved international trade and provided welfare for many including gifting almost 500 orphan girls with dowries to marry so they could escape abject poverty.

Jahinger's memoirs credit her with helping him to live more healthily. Surely someone so intent on seizing control would have given him a shove down the slippery slope of drug dependency. Power-hungry or not, her insightful judgement is not in question as proven when she and Jahinger were held prisoner by a disgruntled general, Mahabat Khan. Whilst in captivity she expertly manipulated the situation to persuade Mahabat's nobles to support Jahinger and Mahabat fled. Unfortunately, Mahabat had the last laugh when Jahinger died soon after this episode. Enlisting the help of Nur's treacherous brother, they moved swiftly to ensure Prince Shah Jahan becomes the next emperor. And here we see the limit of female power, swiftly cut short as soon as her husband dies. They exiled Nur and her daughter to Lahore, where she spent the rest of her life in mourning and relative isolation.

Queen Nzinga
(1581–17 December 1663)

Nzinga is a famous figure in Angolan history. She became the queen of the Mbundu people in the Ndongo Kingdom in 1623 and she was an important symbol in the creation of an independent Angola. In the Portuguese race with other European colonies for land and slaves they had established a fort and settlement in Luanda (Angola's capital) in 1617, land that belonged to the Mbundu. They took many prisoners and forced Ngola (King) Mbande to flee.

In 1622 the Luanda Governor Joao Corria de Sousa invited King Mbande to a peace conference. He sent his sister Nzinga to negotiate instead and she played a blinding move against the Portuguese in their political games. Nzinga entered the room to find the governor sitting on the only chair – a cheap psychological shot. Rather than bow to his intimidation tactics, she made her slave kneel down so she too had a place to park her very important behind. From this equal levelling, she made a deal with the governor that was beneficial to both parties.

However she needed to ally with the Europeans to deal with hostile African neighbours and to secure lucrative trade deals. Nzinga had superb diplomatic, tactical and negotiating skills, and there was an almost Machiavellian touch to her tactics. She understood that converting to Christianity and taking the Portuguese governor's wife's name Anna De Souza would give her greater bargaining power with Europe.

Her sisters converted too and also adopted European names. Later she reverted back to her own native religion only to become Christian again when the political situation demanded it. A veritable Jesus-go-round. She also understood the limitations of being a woman and often dressed in male clothes and demanded to be called king. She was a queen (or king) to be reckoned with.

Of course the governor broke the agreement and Nzinga had to flee a couple of years later.

This was an unlucky break for Queen Mwongo Matamba as Nzinga fled in her direction and conquered her lands, which she swallowed into her kingdom of Ndongo. Meanwhile, a distraught Mbande committed suicide – or did he? – leaving Nzinga in command.

She offered sanctuary to runaway slaves to build her army, allied with the Imbangala tribes and offered alliance to the Dutch in 1641, praising their moral integrity whilst rubbishing their Portuguese enemy – not dissimilar to queen-bee tactics in the school playground of divide and rule. She fought Portuguese colonisation for decades.

Her sisters Mubkumbu Mbande, or Lady Barbara, and Kifunji, or Lady Grace, played an important part in Nzinga's struggles against Portuguese domination. Some sources claim that the sisters were leading advisors and war leaders in the powerful guerrilla army that she created. She employed many women in her council of advisors. Kifunji in particular led a dangerous and thrilling life acting as an undercover spy when she was captured by the Portuguese in 1629. It was the steady stream of intelligence that she sent her sister that enabled Nzinga to play off her enemies so brilliantly. Kifunji was drowned by her enemies in 1647. Frustratingly it's been difficult to find stories about Kifunji's espionage efforts. The Portuguese finally signed a peace treaty with Nzinga in 1657.

Nzinga may have been an important symbol of independence but she was no angel. Some sources believe she kept her own harem of men – oh happy days. Legends abound about her merciless rule such as making the men in her harem fight to the death after she had slept with them – like a designer dress, she only slept with the same man once before going all black widow on them. Powerful women always seem to have sexually murderous and promiscuous gossip attached to them – perchance to discredit?

What is true is that she was ruthless in doing what she considered best for her kingdom including participating in the slave trade as well as happily owning slaves herself. Rumours also abound about her ascension to the throne following her brother's death in 1623. Some sources believe she poisoned him. If she did then she's in good or should we say bad company with half of history's royalty.

Above all Nzinga is held up as a symbol of resistance and independence.

Pauline Bonaparte Borghese
(20 October 1780–9 June 1825)

In character, beautiful Maria Paoletta Buonaparte, aka Pauline Bonaparte, resembles the giddy Lizzie Bennett from Jane Austen's *Pride and Prejudice*. Thoughtless, impulsive, vain, childish, selfish, a romantic predilection for soldiers and a life spent in devout pursuit of pleasure, preferably hers.

She's not a woman to particularly admire or aspire to and she achieved little of consequence. Indeed she is known only for her connection as younger sister (by eleven years) to Napoleon. And yet she is so outrageous and contradictory a figure that it seems unjust not to include her. It must be noted that out of all Napoleon's siblings she was the only one to remain loyal to him.

Her first husband was likely not her first choice, although considering her brother found them in a compromising position, marriage in 1797 was the only option. French Officer Victoire Leclerc, a general in Napoleon's army, was duly given a proper leg up the career ladder and made Governor General of Saint-Domingue (Haiti), where he would die of fever in 1802. Pauline was never faithful to him and had a string of lovers.

Following his death, together with their son Dermide, Pauline returned to France, where Napoleon arranged a second marriage to the equally vain and fickle Italian nobleman Prince Camillo Borghese. Pauline didn't respect him (apparently he wasn't well endowed enough for her) and flirted up a storm around him, behaviour that didn't go down well with her big brother.

> Madame and Dear Sister, – I have learned with pain that you have not the good sense to conform to the manners and customs of the city of Rome; that you show contempt for the inhabitants, and that your eyes are unceasingly turned towards Paris. Although

occupied with vast affairs I nevertheless desire to make known my wishes, and I hope that you will conform to them.

Love your husband and his family, be amiable, accustom yourself to the usages of Rome, and put this in your head, that if you follow bad advice you will no longer be able to count upon me. You may be sure that you will find no support in Paris, and that I shall never receive you there without your husband. If you quarrel with him it will be your fault, and France will be closed to you. You will sacrifice your happiness and my esteem.

However being married into such wealth did have its advantages – Pauline used her riches to help finance some of her brother's campaigns. She commissioned two statues by renowned sculptor Antonio Canova and promptly scandalised him by insisting on posing nude. The sculptures can be seen at the Borghese Palace in Rome. She detested both of Napoleon's wives Josephine and the later Marie Louise, but proved to be a devoted sister, moving to Elba when Napoleon was sent there in exile. When he was exiled to St Helena after the Battle of Waterloo, Pauline returned to Rome to live in the aptly named Villa Paulina.

The favourite sister of Napoleon Bonaparte died at the age of 44 from a suspected cancerous tumour of the stomach.

Penthesilea, Queen of the Amazons

The daughter of Ares, the Greek God of War, and Otrera, the first Amazon Queen, Penthesilea was the mythological Queen of the Amazons of Asia Minor during the Trojan War.

The Amazons were a legendary race of warrior women that you really, really wouldn't have wanted to get on the wrong side of. Legend has it that they were so dedicated to their warrior craft, that they'd cut off one of their breasts so as to be able to wield a bow better.

Penthesilea was beautiful and wise. Highly skilled in weaponry and a fierce warrior, Roman historian Pliny claims that Penthesilea invented the battle axe. Her story is told in the lost Greek literary epic *Aethiopis*, of which only five lines survive.

Her tale is tempered by tragedy. Whilst out hunting she accidentally killed her sister Hippolyte with (depending on the story you read) either an arrow or a spear. Consumed by grief and regret, she wanted only to die, but as a warrior could only do so honourably in battle. She pledged her support to King Priam of Troy and prepared for battle in the Trojan War alongside her personal guard of twelve fellow Amazons (Antibrote, Ainia, Clete, Alcibie, Antandre, Bremusa, Derimacheia, Derinoe, Harmothoe, Hippothoe, Polemusa and Thermodosa).

Rising early on her first (and last) day of battle, she prepared herself. Determined to redeem her soul, she channelled her rage against Achilles, who had killed the Trojan Prince Hector, and vowed to dispatch him. It must have been one hell of a hand-to-hand fight between two epic warriors, especially considering one was the daughter of the God of War and the other was, apart from his 'heel', immortal.

Ultimately however Penthesilea died at Achilles' hand as he thrust his sword through her breast and impaled her. Removing her helmet, Achilles fell completely in love with her. (Or, as other stories have it, he committed necrophilia and had sex with her corpse.)

Fellow Greek solider Thersites mocked Achilles for his romantic weakness and in a 'Hulk punches Thor' moment, killed him. In revenge for that (you can see where the phrase 'Greek tragedy' comes in handy) Thersites's cousin Diomedes fixed Penthesilea's body to the back of his chariot, dragged it to the Scamander River and unceremoniously dumped it. Achilles retrieved it and returned it to the Trojans for its rightful burial.

Poignantly her name means 'mourned by the people', from the Greek words 'penthos' and 'laos' and her story became a firm favourite amongst Greek vase painters. For Harry Potter fans out there, Virgil referred to her as 'Bellatrix', perhaps the inspiration for the character Bellatrix Lestrange. And for DC comic fans (we salute you), Wonder Woman is a fictional Amazonian heroine.

Phoolan Devi
(1963–2001)

It's not good enough to just chronicle the heroines of history. We need to know history's girls for all the flaws, weaknesses and peculiarities that made them human. Bandit Queen Phoolan Devi was a deeply complex character. Worshipped by the downtrodden lower caste people of India, especially the women, she is a folk hero and was dubbed the Indian 'Robin Hood'. As a bandit she only raided upper caste communities and would then redistribute her spoils to the poor.

However, this Robin Hood had a tinge of Bonnie and Clyde about her. Her raids were vicious and her acts of retribution, on the men who had brutalised her, were savage. Many Indians saw her as a feared and violent criminal, responsible for India's greatest mass killing. It was nicknamed the 'St Valentine's Day Massacre Mark 2', in which she was alleged to have murdered twenty-two men. This is a damning indictment but the back story to her acts of violence make judging her actions morally ambiguous.

In 1963 Phoolan was born in Utter Pradesh to a lower caste family, only one rung up from the wretched Dalit 'untouchable' class. The hierarchical system in India was still very much in play. Similar to many lower caste village girls she was married off ridiculously young at the age of 11 to Putti Lal, a brutal man in his 30s. He repeatedly raped and brutalised her and then threw her back to her parents. In her autobiography Phoolan says her parents rescued her.

Regardless, she was now seen as a disgrace in her village. And then following a dispute with her cousin, who had taken family land, she was arrested after his house was 'conveniently' burgled. She was taken to jail and raped in front of her father. By the time they released her she was considered worse than an 'untouchable', forbidden to drink from the well and thus contaminate it. This made her fair game to the upper caste villagers who used and abused her as they saw fit. She was the ripe old age of 13.

Conveniently Phoolan was kidnapped by the Devi, Indian word for bandits, and was no longer the cousin's problem or the village's disgrace. Ironically things began looking up for her for a few seconds anyway. She fell in love with Vikram Singh Mallah, the second in command, after he killed the leader Babu Singh, who was attempting to rape her. For a brief time the two of them led their outlaw posse on several raids as they surfed their righteous crime wave.

It all ended abruptly when a rival gang, resenting competition especially from a lower caste upstart of a girl, ambushed the couple one night. They killed Vikram and carried Phoolan off to a sickening nightmare. They paraded her naked in the village of Behmai where she was gang raped repeatedly for three weeks until she managed to escape. This was the village that would witness the infamous Indian St Valentine's Day Massacre on 14 February 1981. Following her escape she teamed up with Man Singh, a friend of Vikram's, to form a truly fearsome band of outlaws intent on retribution.

When Phoolan's gang arrived in Behmai, she only found two of the men involved in her rape. Allegedly she shot or ordered the shooting of all the men in the village out of sheer frustration but Phoolan claimed she had no part in it. True or not, a massive manhunt began, which she evaded for two years with help from the lower caste community, until sickness halted her. She negotiated surrender – no death penalty and a prison term of eight years. The authorities agreed then threw her in prison for twelve years without a trial. Who knows how long she may have rotted there if the Chief Minister of Utter Pradesh, a staunch supporter, hadn't successfully appealed for her release.

After prison she carried on her fight for the downtrodden but this time she did it legally winning a seat in India's government as a member of the socialist party in 1996. She was India's marmite though, whilst adored by the people she represented, the middle classes were repulsed by her past. She needed bodyguards 24 hours a day. Despite her protection she was shot dead in 2001 by relatives of those killed in the village massacre.

Above all she was a champion for women at the bottom of social hierarchies. Although illiterate, she narrated her story to two ghost writers so she could speak on behalf of the women lost in those dark depths. She was born into deprivation and she became a queen. A powerful message for India's damned.

Pocahontas
(1596–1617)

CAPTAIN JOHN SMITH SAVED BY POCAHONTAS.

The story of Pocahontas has been hijacked by Disney. Although they depicted her as a fabulous, nature-loving heroine, is it really a plus for woman's history to change someone's story so radically? Not to mention reducing them to a piece of merchandise?

The real Pocahontas may well have been fabulous but flaws make a person real and generally more interesting. What was it really like for her, living at the lowest rung of the ladder, as both a woman and a dispossessed minority in a colonial, male world? Not all singing birds and helpful bunnies one imagines.

So whilst Pocahontas lives in so many people's imagination as a free-spirited peacemaker, she still sits perfectly in a female Native American cliché bubble – an anatomically impossible Barbie doll dressed in suede and feathers. Even without Disney's distortion of her character, it's still difficult to tease out the truth. Information either comes from the viewpoint of male colonial settlers or from the oral story telling of the Mattaponi tribe. These accounts are totally opposing and there is little of Pocahontas's voice. She is always the third person and never the narrator.

Mattaponi oral story tellers agree with Walt that this is a love story, just not one between her and the colonial leader John Smith (she would have been 10 when she met him), but that of a father and daughter. All the historical accounts agree she was a daddy's girl, daughter of the chief of the Powhatan tribe, Wahunsenaca. She is presented as being key to cordial relations with the English – 'The Peace of Pocahontas'.

Some of her story has been cobbled together from John Smith. However he writes several years later after the infamous Powhatan rebellion that slaughtered so many of the Virginian colonists. It can be assumed he had an agenda. His famous story that she placed her head in front of his to prevent the chief slaughtering him has many holes. First 10-year-old girls were not allowed to be present at ceremonies and this particular ceremony was to honour him as chief of the English colonists. The Powhatan tribe had made similar allegiances with other neighbouring tribes to avoid war and they perceived the Virginians as just another tribe. It seems unlikely that a feature of the ceremony was to club the honoree's head in. However at the time he was writing to Queen Anne asking to introduce his 'civilised Indian' Pocahontas and needed to ensure she was sufficiently entertaining.

The whole story of the Virginian colonists and the Powhatan tribe is awash with misunderstandings that have been thoroughly lost in translation. It's unlikely that she brought food and supplies for the starving colonists of her own volition. She was probably sent with envoys as a sign of peace. However, relations with the English deteriorated badly. There was a drought and food was scarce. The colonists raided native settlements frequently and fiercely. During this time Pocahontas married Kocoum, a member of the Patawomeck tribe, and oral history remembers them having a child. She would have been around 14. John Smith had returned to England by now.

The English re-enter her life in 1613 when Captain Samuel Argall, desperate to restore order, kidnapped her and held her life to ransom. According to the colonists, she was brought to Jamestown where she was treated well and converted to Christianity. She was married in 1614 to John Rolfe, an English widower who finally rescued the dying settlement by introducing tobacco crops. They had a son called Thomas.

The Manatoponi remember differently. According to her sister, who was brought to keep her company, Pocahontas was severely depressed, unsurprisingly. She had been raped and when pregnant forced to marry John Rolfe. He needed her to gain access to important tobacco crops. She appeared willing so she did not make things worse for her people. Nevertheless relations improved as the marriage created a kinship allegiance.

The Virginia Company was desperate for more support from England and sent Pocahontas and John to London as proof that they were successful in civilising the 'savages' and converting them to Christianity. English society found her enchanting in much the same way you might find a new exhibit captivating. A sign that Pocahontas was not the willing participant claimed was when they bumped into John Smith and she refused to acknowledge him.

On their way home just before they were about to embark at Gravesend, she grew seriously ill and passed away. What killed her is anyone's guess but some believe she was poisoned having outlived her usefulness. Regardless any peace between the British and the Native Americans died with her.

Policarpa 'La Pola' Salavarrieta
(*c.* 1791–14 November 1817)

The heroine of Colombian independence and a member of the Colombian resistance, Policarpa worked as a seamstress as her cover for being spy with the Revolutionary forces when Spain was fighting to regain control of the colony of New Grenada (now Colombia).

Born in Guaduas, in either 1791 or 1795, depending on which historical source you consult, the daughter of Joaquin Salvarrieta, a merchant, and Mariana de Rios, Policarpa was one of eight children. Her parents, brother Eduardo and sister Maria Ignacia died in the smallpox outbreak in 1802.

In 1817 she moved to Bogotá, which was full of Spanish Royalists keen for General Pablo Morillo, aka 'The Pacificator', to continue his so-called Reign of Terror. 'The Pacificator, Brigadier D. Pablo Morillo, arrived,' wrote the wife of a Bogotá physician in a personal account, 'and immediately began the persecution. He imprisoned all revolutionaries, surprising them at night in their homes . . .'

Using forged identity documents, La Pola moved from house to house, 'working' for the women of Spanish Royalist households, wives and daughters of their officers and soldiers, all the while keeping her ear close to the ground and gathering crucial information to pass on to the resistance. She collected money, made uniforms and hid soldiers. She was a brilliant recruiter, with a keen eye for those wanting to move to the side of the Revolutionaries. Eventually discovered, her execution by Spanish Royalist firing squad for treason was witnessed by a 19-year-old soldier, Jose Hilario Lopez, who went on to become President of the Republic of Colombia (although he saved his own skin on arrest by defecting and joining the Royalist forces).

It seems absolutely certain that Policarpa's tongue was never silenced. One account has Policarpa being led into the square yelling so much to the crowd that the Spanish governor feared that the lesson he was trying to impress on the people would be lost. He gave orders for the drummers to beat louder. Still Policarpa raved on, admonishing the soliders for not turning their rifles on the authorities, berating the firing squad for preparing to shoot a woman. Policarpa was in fact not the first woman to be executed under Morillo's regime of terror. At least five other patriot women, in Cali, Cucuta, Tumaco, Popayan and Charala, had been executed. More would follow. 'Assasins!" Policarpa is said to have shouted. 'My death will soon be avenged.'

Forced to face the wall, hands tied behind her back, she was executed.

There is no record of her birth certificate, although those of her siblings survive. There is an annual holiday of celebration in her honour, the 'Day of the Colombian Woman', she features on Colombian banknotes and there is a statue of her in Bogotá.

Princess Olga
(*c.* 890–969)

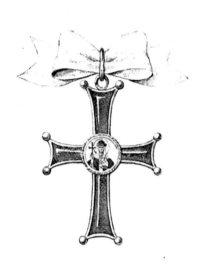

Princess Olga of Kiev ruled from 945–*c.* 963. No one fits the angel-demon cliché more than her. Renowned for burying men alive and setting fire to an entire town because they killed her husband Igor, she somehow was canonised in 1547 as a saint, the first woman in Russia to achieve this accolade.

Kievan Rus (as early Russia was known) at this time was made up of many tribal villages all managed by the capital Kiev. These tribes paid tribute in the form of goods such as furs and honey in an annual trip made by the regent. Unfortunately Prince Igor got a bit greedy and spectacularly underestimated the Slavic Drevlian people. Having already collected tribute, he decided to ask for more – that didn't work out well for Oliver Twist – and the Drevlians killed him for breaking the Viking's equivalent of a gentleman's agreement.

The Drevlians, now a bit cocky, decide to assume power by marrying their leader Prince Mal to Igor's widow Olga, who was now acting regent for her toddler son Sviatoslav (try saying that three times really fast). It was their turn to become victims of woeful underestimation.

Olga pandered to their egos by agreeing to the engagement and asking the delegation to come to Kiev the next day as honoured guests carried in on their boats – a Kiev tradition. Flattered, the delegation retired for the night and as they slept Olga's people dug a giant ditch. The next morning whilst preening like peacocks on their ceremonial boats they were rather dishonourably chucked in the ditch, followed by Olga giving the order to bury them – ALIVE!

Act 2 of Olga's revenge sees her invite Drevlian's VIPs to meet her people to encourage support for the marriage. Innocent of what has befallen their brothers, they duly arrived to be hospitably invited to refresh in the bathhouse.

As soon as they entered, the doors are locked and the bathhouse set on fire, burning them ALIVE! There's a theme emerging.

Still blissfully ignorant of Olga's psychotic acts, the people of the Drevlian capital Iskorosten agree to attend a memorial feast at her husband's grave when she arrives at their capital. Her servants ply them with drink until they are so drunk they barely notice being massacred by her army. Well, they say alcohol numbs pain.

Finally after she invades them with her army, the survivors cotton on that Olga doesn't fancy marriage or indeed any form of alliance and they plead with her to stop, offering their best tributes. She agrees on the proviso they send her three pigeons and three sparrows from every household. Olga orders her people to attach rags drenched in sulphur to the birds' legs and then release them to fly home to their roosts in the Drevlian capital. When the highly flammable sulphur ignites, the town and its people (ALIVE) are burnt to the ground.

All a jolly good yarn to tell little Russians with the light out, but probably heavily embellished having been written down by a couple of monks (who would have loved Stephen King) in *The Tale of Bygone Years* several generations after the devilish deeds were carried out. Although there is no doubt that the Vikings would have demanded some form of ghastly retribution.

Olga was an effective ruler, possibly a lot more than her son proved to be, changing the haphazard and dangerous tribute system into a well-run tax organisation, consolidating the many tribes under her rule and defending the city from the 968 Siege of Kiev whilst Sviatoslav was gallivanting on failed foreign invasion attempts.

All this begs the question – how did such a fiercely independent and ruthless woman become a saint? It seems that after asking to be baptised by the Byzantine Emperor Constantine VII, possibly as a political move to ally with the growing powers of the powerful Byzantine Church, she takes to Christianity like a duck to baptised waters. Constantine also asks to marry her – nothing like the promise of a kingdom to make men want you. She's just not interested and expertly rejects him saying now you are my Christian godfather how can we get married? Luckily he takes it in good humour replying, 'Olga you have outwitted me.'

She can't persuade her son and his subjects to convert but she has such an influence on her grandson little Vladimir that when he assumes power he successfully christanises Kievan Rus. The Church credits her with bringing Jesus to the heathen pagans of Russia, thereby saving many souls. Saint Olga is portrayed as looking humble, pious and subservient – you've got to love papal propaganda.

As she had been canonised by this point for introducing Christianity to Russia, the monks probably wanted to proselytise that even the most evil pagans can be redeemed by Christ.

Ruby Bridges
(1954–)

On the morning of 14 November 1960, 6-year-old Ruby Nell Bridges became the first African-American child to attend William Frantz, an all-white elementary school in the American South. She had a military escort and her mother accompanied her. The event would make her an historic and pivotal member of the civil rights movement.

Her parents were sharecroppers and moved to New Orleans when Ruby (born in Tylertown, Mississippi) was 4. Her father found work at a petrol station and her mother took on night jobs in order to make ends meet. Soon Ruby had another sister and two other brothers; they all shared a room in a small apartment.

At that time schools were segregated. Ruby had a kindergarten near her home, but it was for whites only. She instead travelled several miles to attend an all-black school. Her parents were insistent that she take the 'white school' test – a notoriously difficult test to see whether a black child was intelligent enough to attend a white school. Ruby passed.

It was a mere five streets away but on her first day she was driven there accompanied by federal marshals. She spent the entire day in the head teacher's office. Nearly all the parents of the white children had either kept them at home or came to the school to collect them. Heaven forbid their white children be in the company of a black child. Three other 6-year-old black girls (Tessie Prevost, Gail Etienne and Leona Tate) also made history, attending McDonogh No. 19 School.

For that first school year Ruby had a teacher (white) and a classroom all to herself. She learnt alone. The other two students in the school were white, and learned in a separate classroom. The school was effectively still segregated. The school itself lost a large number of pupils; parents withdrew their children either out of disgust for integration or out of fear at the anger expressed by protestors outside the school. Those who allowed their children to remain also faced resentment for supporting integration.

John Updike, who like fellow writer John Steinbeck, watched events unfold at the school and remarked on the rapid decline in the numbers of students at the school, which originally had around 1,000 pupils enrolled. Other consequences were that Ruby's father was fired from his job and her grandparents were forced off the land they had been sharecropping for the last quarter of a century.

These experiences couldn't fail to shape Ruby's life. A civil rights activist, she worked as a travel agent for fifteen years after high school. She married Malcolm Hall, had four sons and established the Ruby Bridges Foundation, dedicated to fighting racial prejudice and promoting tolerance and respect. Unveiled in 2014, there is now a statue of Ruby Bridges outside William Frantz School. US President Bill Clinton awarded Ruby the Presidential Citizen's Medal in 2001.

Sacajawea
(*c.* 1788–1812)

In 1803, and under President Thomas Jefferson, the US conducted the Louisiana Purchase and bought over 800,000 unexplored square miles of land for $15 million from France. Subsequently the Corps of Discovery Expedition set off to map out a route from Missouri and the Rocky Mountains to the Pacific and back again.

Accompanying them on the 1805–6 voyage of discovery was bilingual Shoshone tribe member Sacajawea. She was the only female on the trip. Although ostensibly brought along for her skills as a translator, Sacajawea was also a herbalist, plant expert and guide to the Corps, led by President Jefferson's 29-year-old secretary Meriwether Lewis and his friend and co-captain 33-year-old William Clark. She helped them trade, barter and traverse the unfamiliar terrain.

It is not known how Sacajawea felt or what she said. No one even knows what she looked like. There are also debates on whether she died when the history books claim she did. What is known is that Sacajawea was born in the Lemhi River Valley (now Idaho), and was part of the Lemhi group of the Native American Shoshone tribe.

Kidnapped in 1800, when she was only 12, during a buffalo hunt by rival tribe Hidatsa she was sold as a slave to fur trader Toussaint Charbonneau. She became the second of his wives (like the Native Americans he lived with, he practised polygamy) and soon bore him a son. Just two months after

Jean-Baptiste Charbonneau was born, on 11 February 1805, Sacajawea, with her husband and newborn, joined the explorers.

Historians are wary of attempts to romanticise her story and are likely appalled by her stereotypical Native American depiction in Hollywood movie *Night at the Museum*. The journals of Clark and Lewis and other members of the Corps reveal a cold lack of empathy for Sacajawea; they never agreed on a common spelling for her name and often just called her squaw, Indian woman or Indian girl. Clark referred to Sacajawea as the group's 'token of peace' and noted that he witnessed Charbonneau striking his wife during a meal.

Hugely useful with her knowledge of the terrain, its edible plants and native languages, it was her visible presence on the expedition, as a mother with a young child, that ensured they were welcomed by other Native American tribes they encountered as peaceful explorers rather than as a possible war party. As a group of men they would have been met with aggression and suspicion.

During one of these encounters, with a group from the Shoshone tribe, Sacajawea was actually joyfully reunited with her brother, now Chief Cameahwait, who provided the Corps with horses to cross the Rockies. Despite the reunion (emotional because once kidnapped, a member of the Shoshone tribe was mourned as 'dead'), she left him behind and continued with the explorers.

When a boat they were travelling in, steered by her husband, hit a squall and nearly capsized she kept calm and ensured valuable supplies, equipment, documents and journals were not lost. At the end of the expedition, declared a success in terms of exploration and mapping, though it did not find the fabled Northwest Passage to the Pacific, Charbonneau was given hundreds of acres of land and $500. Sacajawea received nothing.

Together with her husband and son, Sacajawea travelled to St Louis to visit Clark in 1809, when he took custody of 'Pomp' and assumed responsibility for his education. Three years later Sacajawea had a daughter, Lisette and Clark became custodian of both children. Whilst Jean-Baptiste went on to become an explorer himself, little is known of Lisette or whether she even survived infancy.

Sacajawea died, likely of typhoid, on 22 December 1812 at Fort Manuel in what is now South Dakota. She was just 25 years old. An interpretation of what her face might have looked like was minted on a dollar coin in 2000 and there are monuments dedicated to her in Wyoming and Missouri.

Sappho
(620–550 BC)

Little is actually known of this seventh-century BC poet from Lesbos, the island off Greece where she lived. Her work inspired the terms 'sapphic' and lesbian. Despite no hard evidence of her actual sexual preferences, she is often referred to as the first lesbian poet. Much of the rumour stems from her close friendships with three women, Atthis, Telesippa and Megara.

The fact that her name (a woman's name to boot) survives says much about her accomplishments and influence. What we do have of her work has been painstakingly and meticulously put together from tiny fragments. She is also recorded in the *Suda*, the tenth-century Byzantine version of the *Encyclopaedia Britannica*, and we know she married a rich man called Cercylas and had a daughter called Cleis.

The daughter of wealthy aristocrats, with three brothers, Larches, Charaxos and Eurygios, Sappho has a reputation as one of the greatest poets of Antiquity, although maddeningly very few examples of her lyric poetry (so called as it was written to be accompanied by a lyre) survive, perhaps because it proved too scandalous at the advent of early Christianity, which either censored it or burnt it.

Plato called her 'the Tenth Muse', and she was held in such high regard that she would be known only as The Poetess just as Homer was known as The Poet. The Sapphic type of verse would be named after her and more modern poets from Byron to Tennyson would attempt translations of her work, a sign of her lasting significance and influence.

Her poetry focused on love, passion and eroticism but she would also write religious and more personal poems. The only complete poem of hers which survives is 'Hymn to Aphrodite', recorded by Greek literary critic and historian Dionysius of Halicarnassus.

Shirin Ebadi
(21 June 1947–)

Born in Hamadan, Shirin is the first Muslim woman and first person from Iran to win the Nobel Peace Prize. It was awarded to her in 2003 'for her efforts for democracy and human rights' in Iran and her 'struggle for the rights of women and children'.

She was also, at the age of 22, one of the first female judges in Iran. She gained her doctorate in law from Tehran University in 1971, served for four years (1975–9) as president of Tehran's City Court and is the first Iranian woman to be appointed Chief Justice.

Following the Islamic Revolution of 1979 and the overthrow of the Shah of Iran, Islamic clerics took control of the government, led by the Ayatollah. They were quick to do away with rights for women – including their ability to work as a judge. Shirin was forced to step down. Instead she tried to open her own private lawyer's practice – but wasn't allowed to until 1992, three years after the Ayatollah's death.

During a career particularly focused on defending political prisoners, she's been imprisoned, kept in solitary confinement, spied on, banned from practising law, received death threats, had her bank accounts frozen and her Nobel medal confiscated. She's also penned two memoirs and a book, staunchly defended pro-democracy Iranian-American academic Haleh Esfandiari and fought to expose the identities of attackers who murdered students at Tehran University.

Forbes Magazine included her in their 2004 list of the 100 most powerful women in the world. She founded the Association for Support of Children's Rights in 1995 and the Human Rights Defence Centre in 2001. She has two daughters.

Simone de Beauvoir
(1908–86)

When she grew up Simone Lucie-Ernestine-Marie-Bertrand de Beauvoir wanted to be a nun. However she is celebrated as a French feminist icon and remembered for being a writer, activist, existential philosopher and journalist.

Born in Paris to a devout Catholic family, she had an epiphany at the precocious age of 14, when she declared herself an atheist. Thereon she would focus on maths, literature philosophy and the study of existence. Educated at the prestigious Sorbonne from 1926, three years later she met fellow student and philosopher Jean-Paul Sartre. Their friendship and relationship would endure until his death. He did propose marriage – she refused. She wanted to be free. In fact, being remembered or defined solely as one half of a partnership with a man would probably have infuriated her.

Working as a philosophy teacher following the German occupation of France, she was thrown out of her job by the Vichy government. Their loss was literature's gain, as devoid of a job she turned to writing. She's most famous for her 1949 two-volume *The Second Sex*. Widely regarded as the founding stone of the modern feminist movement, it debated female oppression, challenged the accepted patriarchy and questioned what it meant to be a woman. On publication it was an immediate scandalous sensation – selling over 20,000 copies in its first 2 weeks. She received hate mail, much of it graphic, and leading male intellectuals of the day spoke disparagingly to her.

In the Second World War she fought in the French resistance against the Nazis and in later years protested against the Vietnam War.

The relationship between de Beauvoir and Sartre, which endured for over half a century, was not without its own scandals; de Beauvoir would secure young female philosophy students for Sartre to bed and would often join in to make these couplings a threesome. She also had a passionate love affair with Jewish writer Nelson Algren and in her letters to him refers to herself as his 'wife'. She called him the 'the only truly passionate love in my life'.

De Beauvoir fervently believed that in order to fully be a 'woman' those of the 'second sex' should have a job, be intellectually stimulated and fight for social justice. She died in Paris, where she was buried in the Montparnasse Cemetery together with Sartre; 5,000 mourners attended her funeral. The Simone de Beauvoir Society was established in 1981, and holds an annual international conference. In 2017 the group celebrated its twenty-fourth conference in Haifa, Israel.

Queen Sondok or Seondeouk
(606–47)

King Jinpyeong of Silla, the southern kingdom of Korea (then separated into three different kingdoms), had three daughters and no sons – cue the inevitable moaning about no male heir. However Jinpyeong was fairly enlightened about women thanks to Silla's culture that respected women and even allowed for equal matrilineal lines of inheritance, baffling their Confucian Chinese neighbours. So when Jinpyeong favoured Seondeouk as his successor it only upset a few diehard chauvinists, though they would be a constant thorn in her side.

It is generally agreed that her father chose her to inherit his throne because of her vast intelligence. In a popular anecdote her father received a box of peony seeds and a picture of what the flowers would look like in full bloom from the emperor of the Tang Dynsty in China. When Seondeouk, aged just 7, looked at the picture she said the flowers are pretty but would have no scent. Her astonished father asked how she knew and, perhaps rolling her eyes and translated into modern speech, she answered, 'Duh, there's no bees and no butterflies in the picture – it's so obvious.' When the flowers bloomed as predicted King Jinpyeong was confident, with no daddy bias, that his was the smartest little girl.

Unsurprisingly Seondeouk would still face opposition from the diehards that felt the throne needed a male on it as well as enemies outside her borders who did not take her seriously. In a strategic move worthy of the adage 'keep your enemies close' she formed an uneasy alliance with the Tang Dynasty to ward off attacks from her neighbours. At the same time she had the foresight to arrange political marriages between the highbrow of the three Korean kingdoms that would later be crucial in their unification.

Despite the endless fighting, she seems to have been considered a successful monarch bringing culture, literature and the arts, a stronger connection to Buddhism and astronomy to ancient Korea. She built Asia's first astronomical observatory called Cheomseongdae (the Star Gazing Tower). Seondeouk's childhood tutor from Japan was against teaching a female a discipline he considered totally masculine. Astronomy was very important and was considered a divine skill by which the kings were divinely connected to the heavens and could make premonitions by reading the alignment of celestial bodies, the appearance of comets and so on. She was undeterred. Above all she was a common people's queen. By building this tower for others to use Seondeouk took astronomy to the people. She was also known for implementing policies to help the impoverished and provide welfare. She was also celebrated as a powerful shaman and three incredible prophecies are attributed to her: the peonies already mentioned; the story of the white frogs and a vagina; and foretelling her own death. A colony of white frogs was making a racket at a place known as Jade's Gate. Seondeouk interpreted this to mean that her enemies were converging at the Women's Root Valley as Jade's Gate meant vagina and the frogs were fierce soldiers. She sent her loyal general who did indeed find 2,000 Baekje soldiers about to invade. They were soon sent packing.

She may not have won over all the chauvinists but her reign was sufficiently successful that Silla accepted another female monarch following her death, her cousin Queen Jindeok.

Sophie Morigeau
(*c.* 1836/7–1916)

A frontier-woman and pioneer in the wilds of British Columbia, there are no existing or surviving pictures of Sophie. She was born into a family of fur trappers and traders, and was part of the Metis people, Canada's aborigines. She spent her life trading with both white Europeans and her own Indian people.

At 16 she was married to a white man, fellow trader Jean Baptiste Chabotte, but the union didn't last long and there's very little remaining evidence as to why. She left that relationship but had many more, on her terms and when it suited her – but woe betide any man who tried to take advantage of her.

She didn't take any nonsense. Following an accident with a buggy and runaway horse, she amputated her own rib, which had been left sticking out. Enough said. Apart from the fact that she displayed it in her cabin, tied up with a pink bow. Then of course there's the eyepatch, following a brutal run-in with a homicidal tree branch.

Determined to be her own boss and not a stay-at-home wife, she set up business on her own. Alone and fearless, she led a pack train (a line of animals laden with goods, supplies and often bootleg booze) for trading with both natives and Europeans, travelling through mountains, ravines and rivers. During the heady days of the Wild Horse Gold Rush of 1863, Sophie would lead her pack train from Washington and Montana to supply gold miners further north and would spend time at Galbraith's Ferry, later known as Fort Steele, the town that sprang up to accommodate the prospectors. The Wild Horse River would provide nearly $7 million worth of gold during the rush. When Fort Steele closed in 1870 Sophie was one of the first women from British Columbia to claim land for herself – all 320 acres of it, and set up her own trading post, all by her early 30s, hiding gold coins under her mattress. She kept cattle and horses and was known as a generous woman who would help those who needed it. She died at the age of 80.

Soujourner Truth
(*c.* 1797–1883)

Early civil rights activist, social reformer and speaker Sojourner Truth, born Isabella Baumfree, was the first black woman to publicly speak against slavery.

She was born into slavery herself in around 1797 in Swartekill, Ulster County, New York to parents James and Elizabeth Baumfree. Her exact date of birth is not known because slaves weren't considered important enough to have a birth certificate. Her father was a slave from Ghana and her mother, also known as Mau-Mau Bet, was herself the daughter of slaves from Guinea.

The entire family (Isabella was one of around twelve children) belonged to Colonel Hardenbergh and lived at his holdings in Esopus, just under 100 miles from New York City. Following his death, ownership passed to the colonel's son Charles and after his own demise Isabella was sold at auction together with a flock of sheep for $100. She would be sold twice more before settling at the property of John Dumont at West Park, also in New York.

Dumont forbade her to marry the man of her choice, with whom she'd had a young daughter, forcing her instead to marry one of his own slaves; this meant that any children born of the union would also belong to him. When Dumont broke his promise to grant her freedom, she ran away with her baby daughter in 1826 (New York would free all its slaves on 4 July the following year) to the home of a nearby abolitionist family, the Van Wageners, who paid him $20 to secure her freedom. She then proceeded to do something that no one expected from a black slave woman. Upon discovering her son Peter had been illegally sold across state lines to an owner in Alabama, she took the owner to court. That in itself was mind-blowing for the time. Even more so that she won the case and her son's freedom. Peter would later embark on a whaling ship expedition from which he would never return.

Undergoing a profound spiritual awakening, Isabella converted to Christianity and in 1843 changed her name to Sojourner Truth, embarking on a life dedicated to speaking out against slavery and as an advocate for women's rights. She was a powerful orator and although she had never learned to read or write, she dictated her own story to a friend; this was later published as *The Narrative of Sojourner Truth: A Northern Slave*.

An active member of the Underground Railroad, which helped smuggle black slaves to safety, she delivered a famous speech on slavery and women's rights at the Ohio Women's Rights Convention in 1851. Although the address was later called 'Aint I a Woman?', it's highly unlikely Sojourner, from New York and Dutch speaking, gave it that distinctly Southern-style title. No transcript of the speech in its entirety has survived.

She also helped in the Civil War, recruiting young black men to fight on the side of the Unionists; she later met and thanked Abraham Lincoln for his role in ending slavery. She died aged 86 in Michigan and is buried in Battle Creek.

Susan B. Anthony
(15 February 1820–13 March 1906)

Social reformer, civil rights leader, abolitionist and women's rights leader, Susan was born in Adams, Massachusetts into a devout Quaker family devoted to advocating temperance (abstinence from drinking alcohol) and abolitionism. And for the curious amongst you, the 'B' stands for Brownell.

Susan had six brothers and sisters and was born into an era when women were second-class citizens. No voting rights. They couldn't own their own property or keep their wages. But her father took her education seriously; he didn't have faith in the abilities of the local schools, so decided to home-school Susan himself. She eventually embarked on a teaching career to help her family after they went bankrupt during a national financial downturn, before becoming a campaigner for women's suffrage and against slavery and racial prejudice.

Susan managed feminist newspaper the *Revolution*, which was launched in 1868. It's motto was 'Men, their rights and nothing more; women, their rights and nothing less!' She met fellow activist Elizabeth Cady Stanton in 1851 – it was to be a meeting of minds and the start of a long, devoted friendship.

After attending her first women's rights convention in Syracuse Susan joined the women's rights movement and would travel across New York to promote suffrage and abolitionism. She petitioned the legislature, she lobbied, she lectured and she soon became the New York spokesperson or agent for the American Anti-Slavery Association. The two causes would be irrefutably linked for many years.

She famously voted (for Ulysses S. Grant) in the November 1872 elections in Rochester, New York. The only issue was that women weren't allowed to vote. She was arrested, faced trial and had to fork out $100 for her illegal action – but the ensuing publicity and furore helped widen the audience reach for the women's movement. She would continue to travel across the country to fight for suffrage and was alive to see Utah, Colorado and Wyoming allow women the vote. Although she fought for women in California to have the same right, the motion failed.

The American Equal Rights Association, of which Susan was a member, would famously split into two factions – those who wanted to support the 15th Amendment, which would allow black men to finally have the vote, and those who didn't, because it would be at the expense of the women's vote. The schism was so acute that the association would rip apart into two different groups – the National Women's Suffrage Association, established in 1869 by Susan and Elizabeth Cady Stanton, and the American Woman Suffrage Association.

Susan was enraged by the issue, furious that black or white, it was still men who were being given voting rights before women. Interestingly the issue put her directly at odds with another activist, Sojourner Truth, who felt that as long as progress was being made in the right direction, no matter how slow, they shouldn't stop the momentum of change.

Nonetheless, her efforts proved pivotal in pushing the women's movement forward in the nation's consciousness. Susan introduced an amendment to the Constitution in 1878, for people to be allowed to vote, regardless of their gender. It would only be ratified as the 19th Amendment, on 18 August 1920.

She never married, probably because she knew only too well what that legal state would mean for her rights as a woman. Women were finally given the vote fourteen years after she died.

Truganini
(1812–76)

The history of colonisation has never been pretty but when you add penal colonies and convicts to settlers's greed for land and an atmosphere of fear, the experience takes on a chill that makes Antarctica look cosy. Strip down the Tasmanian devil and you find white colonialism at its heart.

Truganini, an indigenous woman from Tasmania, reveals the terrible history of the infamous Black War between 1803 and 1830 and beyond. Added to the abysmal acts committed against her people, her memory was then used by colonists to perpetuate the convenient illusion that Tasmania's aboriginals were extinct. Many people only knew her from a photograph racially described as 'Truganini the last full-blooded Tasmanian Aborigine'. If she was the last, then what does that make Palawan descendants today?

Truganini was born in 1812 in Bruny Island near Hobart. Europeans had been there since the seventeenth century but the decision to make Tasmania a British penal island in 1803 led to a catastrophic situation as the inept system allowed the escape of prisoners (some barely criminal), many victims of trauma themselves, into the Tasmanian hinterland. Furthermore the Europeans brought disease and a cataclysmic death toll followed.

In a series of atrocities committed against the Tasmanians and the ensuing battles between 1803 and 1830, known as the Black War, indigenous people were cut down in their thousands. Horrifying stories recount unimaginable brutality. When the indigenous people retaliated the violence escalated and so Lieutenant Governor George Arthur declared martial law in 1928 and a bounty offering £5 for an adult and £2 for a child.

Truganini had witnessed her mother Thelgelly stabbed to death in front of her, her sisters abducted to Kangaroo Island and probably sold as slaves, her uncle shot and Praweena her fiancé thrown in the river, his hands cut off so he drowned to death, before she was raped.

When the missionary George Robinson arrived in 1829 he proved to be a complex personality. He was determined to end the violence and make peace but he also believed fundamentally in the superiority of white Christians. The first aboriginal he met was called Wooraddy, and he had lost his wife. Robinson played matchmaker and hooked him up with Truganini who he had befriended when she was 18. The couple joined Robinson in what was known as the Friendly Missions where they attempted to build trust with tribes.

Little was achieved because it was decided to remove the remaining aboriginals from the island, ostensibly for their own protection but also to just get rid. Robinson was paid handsomely to persuade Truganini's people to go to Flinders Island in 1830, which they agreed to as a temporary measure.

The camp there was little better than a prison with dreadful conditions and rife with disease. Their numbers plummeted even further. Truganini was appalled at Robinson, who tried to make matters right by taking a small number including Truganini and Wooraddy to Port Philip. However five of them splintered away and turned vigilante. They headed for the whalers camp in the Western Port area possibly because Truganini believed that is where her sisters had been taken. In October 1842, they attacked a miner's cottage and killed two sailors, although Truganini helped the women to safety first.

They managed to evade capture for five weeks before they were apprehended and taken to trial. Aborigines were forbidden from testifying in court so Robinson perjured himself to say the women were unwitting accomplices, saving them from the death penalty. Truganini watched her husband and friend Umarrah hang, the first people executed in Victoria. She was sent back to Flinders Island and then to Oyster Cove near her birthplace where she resumed a traditional lifestyle. She refused to acknowledge Robinson again.

However in a final insult the Victorian community began to show an interest in aboriginal people in much the same way as they enjoyed investigating an extinct species and desecrated their bodies for the purposes of research. Despite Truganini's pleas to respect her body, her skeleton was put on display in Hobart Museum until 1947. She was not cremated until 1976 when her ashes were finally taken home.

As Jewish women we were brought up with the words 'never forget' – as in never forget the atrocities of the Holocaust. Without doubt Truganini's story should also never be forgotten.

The Trung Sisters
(d. AD 43)

Sisters had been doing it for themselves a long time before Aretha Franklin sang her famous anthem.

National heroines in Vietnam with temples and homages dedicated to their rebellious spirit, the Trung sisters were the Mockingjays of Vietnam's own rebellions and encouraged women born centuries later to take up arms in its most famous war against the US.

The daughters of a nobleman and born in the first century AD near Hanoi, Trung Trac and Trung Nhi would become two of Vietnam's most famous war generals as they pushed back the Chinese trying to subjugate their country. They then ruled as queens for a few years, before being ruthlessly put down.

Both the Vietnamese and Chinese history books have misrepresented the Trung sisters. The first initially elevated them to near mythical status but as their society became more patriarchal what swiftly followed was a far less flattering rewrite; the Chinese depicted their battle as a meaningless mockery. Neither are useful for a proper understanding of women's lives in Vietnam at the time, a period that puts the Western world to shame as women enjoyed a level of autonomy not granted to their European sisters until centuries later.

A popular version of the sisters' story tells us that the Vietnamese were suffering under the barbaric rules of the greedy Chinese Emperor To Dinh. Trung Trac's own husband was executed by the Chinese governor for protesting at a raise in taxes. His death has been touted as the *casus belli* for the ensuing rebellion headed by the Trung sisters in AD 39 or 40 which spread across Vietnam. However the suggestion that Trung Trac fought to avenge her husband as a romantic gesture rather than to free her people from tyranny does seem to smack of condescension.

Regardless the sisters raised an army of 80,000, many of whom were women, and drove the Chinese away. China's emperor was compelled to send in the army under his best general, Ma Yuan, to deal with the uprising. Famously the sisters met him astride elephants but the Chinese forces finally defeated them at the Battle of Lang Bac in AD 41.

Embedded in the story of the Trung sisters is the tale, possibly apocryphal, of another fierce woman. According to legend Phung Thi Chinh, who was heavily pregnant, gave birth on the battlefield and then fastened the baby to her back as she carried on fighting. Knowing what most women experience straight after birth, leaking from every orifice, struggling to breastfeed, it's difficult to believe.

The emperor's need to send in a top general ridicules the more biased legends that claim the Chinese warriors turned up naked to the fight causing the blushing Vietnamese women to run away in embarrassment. It's hard to imagine the women being more scared of a horde of hostile penises than a ferocious army, unless all the laughter rendered them incapable.

Vietnamese academics declared that their rebellion failed because the sisters's followers deserted them, knowing an army of women would lose. These particular scholars wrote their versions a few hundred years later, after being educated by the Chinese patriarchal Confucius ideology. The heady days of female equality were long gone by then and men were fiercely embarrassed by this episode, undermining it with ridicule to soothe their battered pride.

Unfortunately after the plucky Trung girls were defeated the Chinese ruthlessly retained tight control over the Vietnamese and the fate of the sisters was lost in myth and misogyny. Some claim they were beheaded, others believe they took their own lives as a traditional honourable death. Either way they live on in the national imagination influencing the spirit of Vietnam's history.

Veronica Franco
(1546–91)

Sixteenth-century Venetian writer and poet Veronica was one of the *cortigiana onesta*, the intellectual courtesans, not to be confused with the lower class *cortigiana di lume*, prostitutes who worked the Rialto Bridge and offered only sex.

According to records, there were over 11,654 prostitutes in Venice, which had a population of 100,000. You can do the maths. It was fairly simple to be considered a prostitute in Venice. If you were single and were dating a couple of men, then you were considered one. Or if you were married but separated and still dating a couple of men you were also a prostitute. They'd have a whale of a time attempting to make a clear distinction today.

It was also considered vulgar for a woman to be intelligent, express or even have her own opinion. No change there then. Venetian courtesans were world famous. Beautiful, sensual, sexy, enrobed in colourful and bright clothing, often with ribbons and bare breasts, and high-clogged shoes, it's fair to say they were a tourist attraction as they beckoned to customers from the windows and Venetian bridges.

Thanks to the wealth and generosity of their patrons, their lives would be one of extremely comfortable luxury and financial security. Although it wasn't all plain sailing, as the risk of contracting syphilis from one of their lovers was a very real threat, both to their health and that financial security.

Courtesans and aristocratic women actually wore very similar clothing and shoes, but there the resemblance ended. The *cortigiana onesta* were well informed, intellectual, articulate and educated — many times more so than the high-bred, more respectable aristocratic women and wives only viewed by society as vehicles of procreation and objects of prestige.

Women like Veronica, who was classically educated alongside her three brothers, could read and write. Politicians and those in power would seek the counsel of these courtesans, ironic considering that women were not allowed to hold any power in the government of the day. The most famous and high-born of Veronica's lovers was King Henry III of France, to whom she dedicated two of her sonnets in *Lettere familiari a diversi* (*Familiar Letters to Various People*). Their relationship is a great example of how a courtesan could, through her affairs with powerful men, effect change and influence in global politics. Veronica embarked on her affair with the king at a pivotal time for her beloved Venice. Its borders threatened by the Turkish, she persuaded him to provide the republic with ships with which to defend itself.

Her writing was supported by the hugely influential Domenico Venier, a Venetian poet, former senator and the head of Venice's largest literary academy. What set Veronica further apart was that she published two volumes of poetry, the *Terze Rime*, in 1575, followed by *Familiar Letters* in 1580. She played music and was part of an artistic 'salon' of thinkers, philosophers and poets.

Veronica was forced to flee her beloved Venice in 1575 because of the plague and lost most of her money and possessions to looting. She came home in 1577 only to face the Inquisition on charges of witchcraft in 1580 for allegedly bewitching her many happy and loyal noble customers. Her first marriage was likely an arranged one, to a doctor, Paolo Panizza. She had six children from different men, only three of whom survived.

Veronica founded a charity for fellow courtesans whilst also writing letters of caution to friends considering entering their daughters into a life like hers. She died penniless in Venice at the age of 47.

Vivian Bullwinkel
(18 December 1915–3 July 2000)

Born in Kapunda, South Australia, Vivian 'Bully' Bullwinkel was rejected from the Royal Australian Air Force because she had flat feet. Instead she enlisted in the Australian Army Nursing Service in 1941 at the age of 25.

Posted to Singapore on the hospital ship *Wanganella*, she joined the 13th Australian General Hospital with forty-three other nurses. As the Japanese invaded Malaya on 8 December 1941 the hospital was repeatedly bombed and forced to work under blackout conditions at night. As the city fell to the Japanese, she was one of the last 300 civilians, British soldiers and nurses to flee the island for Australia on the boat *Vyner Brooke* on 12 February.

But the escape was not to be – after two days at sea, the freighter was spotted by the Japanese and bombed out of the water. Around 150 survivors clung to pieces of wreckage until they were washed ashore on Banka Island, where they were encouraged to surrender. Most of the British soldiers accompanying them were murdered.

Twenty-one of the army nurses, together with an elderly civilian woman, were forced into the sea by their captors. As they waded in Matron Irene Drummond said to them: 'Chin up girls. I'm proud of you and I love you all.' The final words of another nurse were: 'There are two things I hate in life, the Japs and the sea, and today I've got both.'

The women were then gunned down from the behind in cold blood. Bullwinkel, standing towards the end of the line, was the sole survivor, describing the impact of the bullet that went straight through her waist as like the kick of a mule. She survived only by playing dead, lying on the beach for 10 minutes and waiting until the Japanese soldiers had disappeared. She found a surviving British soldier, known only to her as 'Private Kingsley' who was badly wounded and nursed him for twelve days. At risk of starvation they surrendered again to the Japanese. Private Kingsley died soon afterwards.

Bullwinkel didn't tell the Japanese what she had survived on the beach of Banka Island. They would have shot her if they had known. Instead she spent the following three-and-a-half years as a prisoner of war at Palemberg in Sumatra, doing her job as a nurse for prisoners of war.

There had been 65 Australian nurses on the *Vyner Brooke*: 12 died during the Japanese air raid, 21 were massacred on Radji Beach and 32 became prisoners of war.

Vivian presented evidence of war crimes to the Tokyo Tribunal, following which the Japanese officer thought to have ordered the murders committed suicide. Awarded the Order of Australia, the MBE for bravery and the Florence Nightingale Medal, she died at the age of 84 on 3 July 2000, having returned to Banka Island in 1992 to unveil a memorial to her fellow nurses.

Yaa Asantewaa
(*c.* 1840–1921)

Asantewaa, known as Nana Yaa, was the guardian of the Golden Stool (Sika 'dwa), an artefact of such profound importance to the Ashanti nation (modern-day Ghana) it inspired a rebellion against the British known as the War of the Golden Stool. It was led by Nana Yaa in 1900.

Nana Yaa had been appointed by her brother the ruler (Eijushne) of the Ejisu as their Queen Mother, a powerful position that enabled her to have her grandson appointed Eijushne when her brother died in 1894. When the British colonial powers exiled her grandson alongside King Prempeh II of the Ashanti Empire in 1896 she ruled in his stead over the Ejisu-Juaben District.

Although the British helped Prempeh win a bitter civil war he was damned if he would let them trample over his people, land and traditions, although he was happy to remain friends. However the British were firmly ensconced on the Gold Coast swiping the Ashanti gold mines and trying to convert all and sundry to Christianity. Prempeh's success as a leader made the colonists nervous and after he refused to give up his independence, they exiled him and several supporters to the Seychelles.

Governor Frederick Hodgson didn't think it was enough to take away the Ashanti's beloved leader, he demanded that they recognise him, and per se Britain, as the rightful ruler. He knew whoever owned the stool owned the land.

Each Asantahene (king) assumed his power after taking part in a sacred ritual of the Golden Stool. Tradition told that in the seventeenth century the stool had fallen from the sky onto the lap of the first king of the Ashanti Empire, Osei Tutu. Priest Okomfo Anokye revered for his divine powers declared that the soul of the Ashanti kingdom resided in the stool and its loss would signal the destruction of the Ashanti kingdom.

At first only Yaa stood up to Hodgson. In a famous secret meeting held by the Ashanti to discuss Hodgson's demands, the men wanted to give in. Yaa stood up and made a famous speech in which she chastised them for their lily-livered cowardice, and like many women before her and since she said if the men won't do the job the women will even if it means fighting to their deaths.

And she was true to her word leading the Ashanti in rebellion with 20,000 supporters. She reportedly threatened the women to withhold sex until the men joined the fight. The British thought they would quell the rebellion quickly but Yaa's clever strategies meant it took several months. She besieged the fort of Kumasi. After the British had to call in extra troops they were still unable to capture Yaa. It was only after hearing of her grandchildren's capture that she handed herself in. She was sent to join Prempeh in June 1901 and she died in exile.

It was a spiritual victory as the British never got hold of the Golden Stool and the people never stopped believing that Prempeh was their rightful king. He was returned from exile after years of petitioning inside and outside Ghana.

Yaa's bravery and resolution inspired the Ashanti people who would never give up seeking independence. Their dream was finally realised in 1957.

The Unknown Woman

I am your ancestor. I am everyone's ancestor, the one history never considered significant enough to record or important enough to educate so that I might leave behind diaries of my own.

I am a street girl from Brazil; a homeless woman from India; an indigenous tribal leader from the 'new world'; a prostitute from Thailand.

I am the peasant thrown in an unmarked grave; the midwife and wise woman persecuted for being a witch, whose healing skills were lost to the patriarchy of medicine; an artist, sculptor and musician whose talents were neither given training nor recognition. I am just the mother, sister, daughter whose small acts of heroism and bravery will never be known – the housewife who shielded the persecuted in war or fed the starving during crisis.

Maybe I was a rebel, a heroine or a villain but only the lucky or truly unusual have been given the rare honour of memory. I shouldn't need to be a hero to have a name and identity.

I am many and I am none for I have no name.

There is his story and there is her story and without both of them we will never know the true story.

Photo Sources

1. Ada Blackjack

www.nunatsiaqonline.ca

2. Agent 355

www.nwhm.org
www.ladiesindefiance.com
www.womenhistoryblog.com
www.biography.com
www.allthingsliberty.com
www.nwhm.org

3. Agostina Domenech

John Lawrence Tone, 'Spanish Women in the Resistance to Napoleon' in Constructing
Spanish Womanhood: Female Identity in Modern Spain
The Mirror of Literature, Amusement, and Instruction, Volume 41, 1843, John Timbs
(b. 1801-d. 1875)
History of the Peninsular War by Robert Southey (b. 1774- 1843), Esq. LL. D. Poet ...,
Volume 1

4. Anne of Cleves

www.en.wikipedia.org

5. Aspasia of Miletus

www.livius.org
www.historywiz.com
penelope.uchicago.edu

6. Aud/Unn or Audunn The Deep Minded

www.iamnotthebabysitter.com
www.historyextra.com
www.equest4truth.com

7. Audrey Hepburn

www.pixabay.com

8. Azucena Villaflor

en.gariwo.net

www.ipsnews.net

www.articles.latimes.com

www.truth-out.org

www.lab.org.uk

9. Calamity Jane

commons.wikimedia.org

10. Cartimandua

www.britishmuseum.org

11. Catherine the Great

www.livescience.com

www.bbc.co.uk

www.history.com

www.biography.com

12. Ching Shih

commons.wikimedia.org

13. Christina of Sweden

annabelfrage.wordpress.com

14. Cixi

www.en.wikipedia.org

15. Cleopatra

www.smithsonianmag.com

16. Coco Chanel

commons.wikimedia.org

17. Edith Cavell

McFadyen, Rev Phillip and Chamberlin, Rev David, "Edith Cavell 1865-1915 – A Norfolk Heroine" 1985, 1997- 2015. www.edithcavell.org.uk (Accessed 20th March 2017)

www.telegraph.co.uk

historysheroes.e2bn.org

18. Eliza Josolyne

www.wellcomeimages.org

19. Eliza Ruhamah Scidmore

www.agreatblooming.com

intelligenttravel.nationalgeographic.com

news.nationalgeographic.com

www.washingtonpost.com

www.britannica.com

www.nps.gov

20. Dame Emma Hamilton

www.emmahamiltonsociety.co.uk

www.bbc.co.uk

www.npg.org.uk

21. Empress Theodora

https://www.britannica.com/biography/Theodora-Byzantine-empress-died-548

Full image reference: https://www.metmuseum.org/art/collection/search#!?q=empress%20

theodora&perPage=20&sortBy=Relevance&sortOrder=asc&offset=0&pageSize=0

Short image link: www.metmuseum.org/art

22. Empress Wu Zetian

www.en.wikipedia.org

23. Flora Sandes

commons.wikimedia.org

24. Golda Meir

jwa.org

25. Gorgo

www.ancient.eu/Gorgo_of_Sparta/

26. Grace Humiston

www.thehistoryreader.com

27. Gráinne Ní Mháille, aka Grace O'Malley, Queen of Umail and Pirate Queen of Ireland

commons.wikimedia.org

28. Gracia Mendes Nasi

jwa.org

forward.com

29. Harriet Beecher Stowe

www.harrietbeecherstowecenter.org/utc/

30. Hatshepsut

www.metmuseum.org/art

31. Hedy Lamarr

commons.wikimedia.org

32. Hester Stanhope

archive.aramcoworld.com

33. Huda Shaarawi

Image: commons.wikimedia.org

34. Hypatia

Sources: "Hypatia, Ancient Alexandra's Great Female Scholar," by Sarah Zielinski, Smithsonian Magazine, March 15, 2010

commons.wikimedia.org

35. Ida and Louise Cook

i.telegraph.co.uk

36. Isabel Godin des Odonais

www.labrujulaverde.com

37. Isabella of France, Queen of England

edwardthesecond.blogspot.co.uk

38. Dr James Barry

Nightingale, Florence. *Letter to Parthenope, Lady Verney (undated)*. London: Wellcome Institute for the History of Medicine.

39. Jeanie Cameron of Glendessary, West Highlands

40. Jezebel, Queen of Israel
commons.wikimedia.org

41. Kalpana Chawla
commons.wikimedia.org

42. La Malinche aka Mallinali, aka Dona Marina
commons.wikimedia.org

43. Lili Elbe and Gerda Gottlieb
wellcomeimages.org

44. Lilith (A Long Time Ago In a Garden Far, Far Away)
commons.wikimedia.org

45. Lucretzia Borgia
www.historytoday.com
www.biography.com
www.nationalgeographic.com
www.historychannel.com.au
thehairpin.com

46. Lucy, or AL 288-1
commons.wikimedia.org

47. Luisa Casati
commons.wikimedia.org

48. Madame du Barry
www.metmuseum.org/art

49. Madam Sacho
s-media-cache-ak0.pinimg.com

50. Madam Stephanie Queen St Clair
www.themobmuseum.org

51. Madeleine de Verchère

commons.wikimedia.org

52. Marie Antoinette

commons.wikimedia.org

53. Marie Marvingt

commons.wikimedia.org

54. Mariya Oktyabrskaya

s-media-cache-ak0.pinimg.com

55. Mary Anning

http://www.lymeregismuseum.co.uk

56. Mary Edmonia Lewis

Source: The Indomitable Spirit of Edmonia Lewis. A Narrative Biography: © 2012
A.K.H. All rights reserved.

www.americanart.si.edu

www.aljazeera.com

www.smithsonianmag.com

www.encyclopedia.com

57. Mary Frith aka Moll Cutpurse

commons.wikimedia.org

58. Mary Seacole

commons.wikimedia.org

59. Mary Shelley and the ghosts of Fanny Imlay and Harriet Shelley

commons.wikimedia.org

60. Mary Wilcocks, aka Princess Caraboo

commons.wikimedia.org

61. Mary Wollstonecraft

commons.wikimedia.org

62. Mata Hari, or Margaretha Zelle

commons.wikimedia.org

PHOTO SOURCES

63. Maw Broon

100 Women Images\Maw Broon.jpg
Maw Broon ® © DC Thomson & Co. Ltd. 2017
Used by Kind Permission of DC Thomson & Co. Ltd.

64. Maxine Elliot

commons.wikimedia.org

65. Messalina

commons.wikimedia.org

66. Mileva Maric

blogs.scientificamerican.com
www.livescience.com
bnrc.berkeley.edu
www.onthisdeity.com
www.openculture.com

67. Mirabal Sisters

download.fotolia.com

68. Moremi Ajaso

https://lifestyle.thecable.ng/moremi-ajasoro-ile-ilfe-tallest-statue/

69. Nanny and the Maroons

www.eachoneteachone.org.uk

70. Neerja Bhanot

images.catchnews.com

71. Nur Jahan or Mehr-un-Nisa

commons.wikimedia.org

72. Queen Nzinga

commons.wikimedia.org

73. Pauline Bonaparte

D.A. Bingham, A Selection from the Letters and Despatches of the First Napoleon, Vol.
II (London, 1884), p. 70.

74. Penthesilea, Queen of the Amazons

www.ancient-origins.net

75. Phoolan Devi

snusercontent.global.ssl.fastly.net

76. Pocahontas

commons.wikimedia.org

77. Policarpa 'La Pola' Salavarrieta

Notable Latin American Women: Twenty-nine Leaders, Rebels, Poets, Battlers , Jerome R. Adams

78. Princess Olga

commons.wikimedia.org

79. Ruby Bridges

www.nola.com

80. Sacajawea

hilo.hawaii.edu

www.biography.com

81. Sappho

www.poetryfoundation.org

departments.kings.edu

www.adnax.com

www.newyorker.com

82. Shirin Ebadi

https://nobelwomensinitiative.org/laureate/shirin-ebadi/

83. Simone de Beauvoir

www.famous-trials.com

www.spiegel.de

84. Queen Sondok or Seondeouk

commons.wikimedia.org

PHOTO SOURCES

85. Sophie Morigeau

Recollecting: Lives of Aboriginal Women of the Canadian Northwest and ..., edited by
Sarah Carter, Patricia Alice McCormack
100 More Canadian Heroines: Famous and Forgotten Faces
By Merna Forster
www.rejectedprincesses.com

86. Soujourner Truth

https://www.biography.com/people/sojourner-truth-9511284

87. Susan B Anthony

www.womeninworldhistory.com
www.famous-trials.com

88. Trugianini

commons.wikimedia.org

89. The Trung Sisters

znews-photo-td.zadn.vn

90. Veronica Franco

www.ancientdigger.com
Margaret F. Rosenthal. The Honest Courtesan: Veronica Franco, Citizen and Writer in
Sixteenth- Century Venice (Chicago: The University of Chicago Press, 1992)

91. Vivian Bullwinkel

commons.wikimedia.org

92. Yaa Asantewaa

commons.wikimedia.org

93. The Unknown Woman

static.pexels.com